SOUTH-WESTERN

ENTREPRENEURSHIP

STARTING YOUR OWN BUSINESS

Dr. Roger Hutt
Coordinator,
Undergraduate Business Programs
Arizona State University West

Managing Editor: Robert E. Lewis
Developmental Editor: Willis S. Vincent
Production Manager: Carol Sturzenberger
Senior Production Editor: Mark R. Cheatham
Production Editors: Mark D. Beck/Marianne Miller/Nancy Shockey
Senior Marketing Manager: Dick Walker
Designer: Nicola M. Jones
Photo Researcher: Kimberly A. Larson

Credits for Cover Photos: SUPERSTOCK; T. Rosenthal/SUPERSTOCK; Photo Courtesy of Hewlett-Packard Company; Allied-Signal, Inc.

Credits for Entrepreneur Photos: Wal-Mart Stores, Inc., 1; The ASK Group, Inc., 25; McDonald's Corp., 55; © Mrs. Fields, Inc., 83; © Ed Kashi, 109 (both photos); Courtesy of Johnson Publishing Company, Inc., 139; Courtesy International Bank of Commerce, 165; Courtesy Lillian Vernon Corp., 185.

ISBN: 0-538-62088-9

1 2 3 4 5 6 DH 98 97 96 95 94 93

Printed in the United States of America

PREFACE

An entrepreneur is a person who attempts to earn a profit by taking the risk of operating a business enterprise. Thousands of people become entrepreneurs each year. They start their own businesses from scratch, buy existing businesses, or buy franchised businesses. If they are successful in providing products and services to consumers at a profit, they will build rewarding careers for themselves as entrepreneurs. This text-workbook will help students understand what it is like to be an entrepreneur and what is involved in starting a business.

Entrepreneurship: Starting Your Own Business is written to enable students in a wide variety of classes to study entrepreneurship. Approximately 35 to 40 clock hours of instruction are required to cover the text material and learning activities. The text-workbook is designed to (1) introduce students to the concept of entrepreneurship, (2) present entrepreneurship as a career path that is worthy of consideration, and (3) provide students with a realistic framework for starting their own businesses.

ORGANIZATION OF CHAPTERS

Entrepreneurship: Starting Your Own Business is organized into eight chapters, each of which develops a topic important for prospective entrepreneurs.

CHAPTER 1, "Discovering the World of Entrepreneurship," provides basic facts about entrepreneurship, introduces the major fields of business activity, including international trade, and sets the stage for preparing a business plan.

CHAPTER 2, "Examining Entrepreneurship as a Career," deals with the advantages and disadvantages of working for oneself, describes types and characteristics of successful entrepreneurs, focuses on personal financial needs, and compares the ways of going into business.

CHAPTER 3, "Using Your Creativity," develops an understanding of how creativity is used to find ideas for new enterprises and to operate businesses more efficiently.

CHAPTER 4, "Analyzing Markets and Competitors," introduces the concepts of sales forecasts and business location and suggests ways to study the competition.

CHAPTER 5, "Planning a New Enterprise," covers ways of defining the business, legal forms of business enterprise, organizing the work of the enterprise, family-owned business issues, and sources of assistance.

CHAPTER 6, "Marketing the Product or Service," is an overview of marketing, presenting a discussion of types of products and services, channels of distribution, pricing, personal selling, advertising, and sales promotion and including a discussion of business ethics.

CHAPTER 7, "Obtaining Financing," examines types and sources of funds for starting a business, factors in the need for additional capital, and tips for requesting loans.

CHAPTER 8, "Preparing the Financial Plan," deals with preparing financial statements and shows how changes in price, volume of sales, cost of sales, and operating expenses affect profit.

FEATURES

Entrepreneurship: Starting Your Own Business contains the following features to help students learn the subject matter:

1. **Realistic learning objectives** are stated at the beginning of each chapter.
2. The **entrepreneur profile** at the beginning of each chapter describes the career of a successful entrepreneur.
3. **Key business terms** are printed in bold italics in the text when they are being defined for the first time.
4. **Examples** are based on smaller businesses, especially those from which students frequently buy products and services.
5. Each chapter ends with a highlighted section titled **Action Steps for Aspiring Entrepreneurs,** a set of steps to help students prepare for the possibility of being entrepreneurs at some point in their careers.
6. Five categories of carefully selected **learning activities** are included at the end of each chapter:

Building Your Enterprise Vocabulary. Students demonstrate their knowledge of important terms by matching a term with its definition or application.

Understanding Key Concepts. By writing answers to questions, students indicate their comprehension of concepts related to entrepreneurship.

Applying Your Enterprise Knowledge. When given the description of a specific incident or situation, students will apply what they have learned in the chapter.

Solving Business Problems. In writing their solutions to these case problems, students have the opportunity to use their problem-solving skills.

Business Plan Project. This project is the thread that runs through the entire text-workbook. When students have completed the Business Plan Project sections in all eight chapters, they will have complete business plans for enterprises of their choice.

TEACHER'S EDITION

The teacher's edition of *Entrepreneurship: Starting Your Own Business* consists of the following five sections:

Section I explains the organization of the text-workbook, provides suggestions for using the text-workbook, and lists selected references.

Section II contains for each chapter learning objectives, an objectives matrix, and teaching suggestions.

Section III provides transparency masters for each chapter.

Section IV consists of a 25-item chapter test (10 true/false, 10 multiple-choice, and 5 short-answer questions) and a final examination consisting of 50 questions (20 true/false, 20 multiple-choice, and 10 short-answer). Answers to these tests are given at the end of the section.

Section V is a sample business plan project.

VIDEO AND MANUAL PACKAGE

The videotape *Entrepreneurship in Action* correlates with the text-workbook and explores six topics: (1) Finding a Place in Entrepreneurship, (2) Choosing a Business to Start, (3) Organizing a Business, (4) Understanding Markets and Competitors, (5) Marketing Products and Services, and (6) Financial Planning. Suggestions for integrating the concepts developed in the videotape into classroom instruction are included in an accompanying manual.

MESSAGE TO THE STUDENT

Your study of entrepreneurship will be important to you for these reasons:

1. Entrepreneurship is important to our nation's economy. Entrepreneurs have a remarkable record of creating and bringing to the market new and improved products and services. Some of today's new, small companies will be tomorrow's large companies employing hundreds or even thousands of people.
2. You may find that you want to become an entrepreneur. This career offers exceptional opportunities for people who work hard and who find new and better ways to serve the needs and wants of their customers.
3. Even if you do not become an entrepreneur, your knowledge of entrepreneurship may help you in the career you select. Entrepreneurs are among the most important customers of many types of business firms and professional practices. For example, as an accountant, lawyer, or banker, you may help entrepreneurs start their businesses. As a sales representative for a large company or as

an insurance agent, you may find that a large number of your customers are entrepreneurs.

Entrepreneurship: Starting Your Own Business is based on the author's experience in helping students learn about entrepreneurship and in advising people who start businesses. May this experience, which is reflected in this text-workbook, guide you through your study of entrepreneurship.

ROGER W. HUTT

CONTENTS

CHAPTER 1

DISCOVERING THE WORLD OF ENTREPRENEURSHIP

One of the freedoms you enjoy in the United States is the freedom to choose how you will earn a living. Some people choose to work for others in stores, factories, schools, or hospitals. Other people choose to work for themselves in their own businesses. The opportunity to be in business for yourself is one of the characteristics of American life. This chapter will introduce you to entrepreneurship, the process of starting a business.

Learning Objectives

After you have studied Chapter 1, you should be able to:

1. Define entrepreneurship.
2. Distinguish between entrepreneurship and small business management.
3. Identify the major fields of business activity.
4. Describe the growing importance of international business.
5. Discuss the future prospects for entrepreneurship.

ENTREPRENEUR PROFILE Sam Walton

Sam Walton's life of hard work, combined with his education and the entrepreneurship skills he developed at an early age, helped him to become a respected businessman and the richest man in America. He made his fortune from the Wal-Mart store chain, the business he started in 1962.

As early as his freshman year in high school, Sam Walton showed that he was hard-working and ready to seize an opportunity. After milking the family cow, and making sure his family had enough milk, he bottled what was left and sold it in the neighborhood. He also earned his own spending money by doing odd jobs, delivering newspapers, and working part-time in a five-and-ten-cent store. To pay his way through college, Sam continued delivering newspapers and waited tables at the university in exchange for his meals.

Sam Walton graduated from the University of Missouri in 1940 with a degree in economics. After deciding that retailing might be a good career path to follow, he accepted a job with the J. C.

Penney Company, a firm known for its emphasis on customer satisfaction. He was assigned to the store in Des Moines, Iowa, as a management trainee and salesperson. Sam saw this job as an opportunity to learn retailing from one of the top firms in the business.

Sam had to interrupt his retailing career to serve in World War II as an Army officer. Upon returning to civilian life in 1945, Sam went back to retailing, but not to J. C. Penney. With his brother, Bud, he obtained a franchise to operate a Ben Franklin variety store in Newport, Arkansas, a town of about 4,000 people. When the opportunities arose, the Walton brothers bought variety stores in the small towns nearby and, by the early 1960s, had become the most successful Ben Franklin franchisees in the country.

A relatively new concept in retailing, discount merchandising, was sweeping the country during the 1950s and the early 1960s. Sam and Bud were eager to convert their franchised outlets to this new type of retailing. Before they could do this, however, they needed approval from Ben Franklin executives. In 1962, Sam traveled to Chicago to convince the executives to allow discount-merchandising practices in the stores. When they refused, he ended his relationship with the company and pursued the opportunity on his own.

Sam opened his first Wal-Mart general merchandise discount store in Rogers, Arkansas, in 1962. Additional stores have been built over the years, with the first ones being limited to small towns; locations in larger cities were acquired later. Always alert for new ways to increase business, Sam paid attention to business growth factors and areas of opportunity. Both of these topics are discussed in Chapter 1.

Two new concepts in the 1980s caught Sam's attention. One was the warehouse club store and the other was the hypermarket. Both of these new concepts were added to the Wal-Mart organization. The first Sam's Wholesale Club was opened in 1983. In partnership with a Texas food wholesaler, the first Hypermarket USA was opened in 1987.

Sam's Wholesale Club consists of a warehouse-type building in which customers, who must first buy a membership, select their purchases from cartons or from shipping pallets. Among the items carried are office equipment, automobile tires, microwave ovens, canned goods, and frozen meats. Small business owners and individual consumers are eligible for membership.

Hypermarket USA is a one-stop superstore occupying about 200,000 square feet of space. To get some idea of what this superstore is like, imagine a shopping center without the interior walls. You will find a complete line of supermarket, apparel, general merchandise, and furniture items. Without leaving the store, you also have access to a bank, a dry cleaner, a hairstyling salon, and a number of other services.

Observers believe that Wal-Mart's fast growth has been due in large part to Sam Walton's willingness to seize opportunities and to pursue his dream. Perhaps Sam's retailing dream can be described best by the following table, which shows how the company has grown in terms of both number of stores and sales volume:

Year	Number of Stores	Annual Sales
1962	1	$700,000
1970	38	$30,000,000
1980	330	$1,200,000,000
1990	1,528	$25,800,000,000

The 1,528 stores in 1990 consisted of 1,402 Wal-Mart discount stores, 123 Sam's Wholesale Clubs, and 3 Hypermarket USA stores. These three types of stores are examples of over-the-counter retailing, which is discussed in Chapter 1.

Sam Walton chose to work for himself and operate his own business. He went to work every day until his death at age 74 in 1992.

Source: Vance H. Trimble, Sam Walton: The Inside Story of America's Richest Man *(New York: Dutton, 1990), and John Huey, "America's Most Successful Merchant,"* Fortune *124, no. 7 (September 23, 1991): 46–59.*

THE ROLE OF ENTREPRENEURSHIP

Each year thousands of individuals launch new business enterprises. By meeting the needs and wants of consumers, they build rewarding careers for themselves as entrepreneurs.

WHAT IS A BUSINESS ENTERPRISE?

An establishment that supplies us with products and services in exchange for payment is referred to as an ***enterprise,*** a ***business,*** or a ***business enterprise.*** America depends on thousands of entrepreneurs to supply the products and services everyone needs. ***Products,*** also called ***goods,*** are tangible items—things you can touch such as clothing, furniture, and cosmetics. ***Services*** are tasks we pay others to do or provide for us. Services are intangible, which means that you cannot touch them. Examples of using services include calling a plumber, going to a hairstylist, taking dancing lessons, or taking your automobile to a mechanic for repair.

WHO IS AN ENTREPRENEUR?

An ***entrepreneur*** (än′ trə prə nėr′) is a person who attempts to earn a profit by taking the risk of operating a business enterprise. If you start a business, or buy one that someone else started, you are an entrepreneur. In the past, only individuals who created new types of businesses were called entrepreneurs. Examples are Henry Ford, Edwin Land, Frederick W. Smith, Steven P. Jobs, and Stephen Wozniak. Henry Ford started the Ford Motor Company in 1903, when automobiles were still new to most people. Edwin Land founded the Polaroid Corporation in 1937 with his invention of the world's first polarizing sheet material. Then in 1948, he began distributing another of his inventions—the Polaroid instant camera. Frederick W. Smith introduced a revolutionary overnight package delivery service when he started Federal Express Corporation in 1973. Steven P. Jobs and Stephen Wozniak teamed up to develop a microcomputer and to start Apple Computer, Inc. They introduced their first microcomputer, the Apple I, in 1976, followed by the popular Apple II model in 1977.

WHAT IS ENTREPRENEURSHIP?

Entrepreneurship is the act or process of getting into and managing your own business enterprise. It is easy to understand why starting a business from scratch is entrepreneurship, but why is the term used when people buy either existing businesses or franchises? Because these people also take risks, invest money and energy, and apply their own creativity and ingenuity to the business. They are responsible for the success of their business ventures even though they were not the founders.

Entrepreneurs spend a lot of their time organizing, managing, and assuming responsibility for their enterprises. ***Organizing*** is the process of gathering the money, people, and machinery needed to get the business started. ***Managing*** involves seeing to it that the day-to-day tasks are performed appropriately. ***Assuming responsibility*** means making sacrifices for the enterprise. This may include working twelve hours a day and having little time to spend with family and friends. It may require going without a paycheck for weeks or months. However, once the business is successful, the entrepreneur will profit from these efforts.

Illustration 1-1
Part of running a business is seeing that the day-to-day tasks are performed appropriately.

Most new enterprises start small and have these key features:

1. The owner is the manager.
2. The owner supplies most of the money to start the enterprise.
3. The business is usually local, serving the immediate community and nearby towns. (There are exceptions; for example, small mail-order firms may ship goods all over the country.)

HOW DO ENTREPRENEURSHIP AND SMALL BUSINESS MANAGEMENT DIFFER?

Entrepreneurship and small business management are separate yet related terms. Entrepreneurship refers to the act or process of getting into and managing a business enterprise. It is the source from which all businesses, both large and small, spring. On the other hand, a ***small business*** is one that is independently owned and operated and is not one of the major companies in its field of business activity. The process of operating a small business is known as ***small business management.***

WHY STUDY ENTREPRENEURSHIP?

The study of entrepreneurship is important to you for these reasons: (1) it may lead you to a satisfying career; (2) it can help you become a better-informed citizen; and (3) it may help you in dealing with customers who are entrepreneurs.

TO EXPLORE CAREER OPPORTUNITIES. People study entrepreneurship to see what it takes to start a business. They want to learn how they can change an idea, a recipe, or their flair for fashion into a career. Of all the people who dream about being their own bosses, more than 2,000 achieve that dream each day by launching their own enterprises.[1] Ask yourself this question when thinking about your career: Why not start a business?

TO BECOME BETTER INFORMED. The United States is a nation of small businesses. Nearly 70 percent of the enterprises are owned by only one person.[2] In many cases, there are no employees other than the owner. Enterprises with fewer than 100 employees account for nearly three-fourths of the existing jobs and for many of the new jobs created each year.[3] Entrepreneurs, therefore, play an important role in America, yet many citizens know very little about them.

TO LEARN ABOUT POTENTIAL CUSTOMERS. Small businesses are often customers for other business firms. For example, insurance salespersons call on business owners (entrepreneurs) to sell fire, medical, and other insurance policies. Architects plan new commercial buildings and assist with remodeling. Various manufacturers provide items needed by small businesses such as computers, sales registers, calculators, machinery, and supplies. Other examples are loan officers in banks who process small business loans; advertising salespersons for newspapers and radio stations who call on small businesses; and real estate agents who sell and lease business property.

---

1. U.S. Small Business Administration, *Handbook of Small Business Data 1988* (Washington, DC: U.S. Government Printing Office, 1988), 7.
2. Ibid.
3. U.S. Small Business Administration, *The State of Small Business: A Report of the President* (Washington, DC: U.S. Government Printing Office, 1989), 48.

WHAT IMPORTANT ROLES DO SMALL BUSINESSES PERFORM?

Small business firms are an important part of American business because they (1) distribute to consumers most of the products made by large manufacturers, (2) provide goods and services to big businesses, (3) generate ideas for new goods and services, (4) perform certain services better than larger firms, and (5) keep consumer products in working order.

DISTRIBUTE TO CONSUMERS. Even when a product is manufactured by a large company, there is a good chance that it will be sold to the consumer by a small business. Automobiles, for example, are manufactured by large corporations located in the United States and in other countries. However, cars are sold to the public through auto dealerships. Many of the 28,000 dealers for new cars and trucks in this country are small businesses.[4] Products of other giants of American industry, such as the Procter & Gamble Company, the Black & Decker Corporation, and PepsiCo, Inc., are available for sale in thousands of small stores throughout the country. Procter & Gamble's 160-plus products include laundry detergents, toothpaste, and food and beverage items. Black & Decker manufactures power tools, indoor and outdoor appliances, and hardware items. In addition to Pepsi, PepsiCo's products include other soft drinks and a line of snack foods.

DISTRIBUTE TO BIG BUSINESS. Small businesses provide goods and services to big businesses. Parts for automobiles, airplanes, radios, and televisions, to name just a few products, are manufactured by small enterprises.[5] Likewise, just over 1,000 costume jewelry makers and more than 2,700 producers of toys and sporting goods stand ready to provide their products to retailers such as Wal-Mart, Dillard's, or J. C. Penney stores.[6]

DEVELOP NEW IDEAS. America depends on small businesses for inventions that lead to new and better products. Many products of today came about because an entrepreneur saw a need and searched for a way to meet it. Individuals or small firms invented power steering for automobiles, FM radio, aerosol cans, air conditioning, dry chemical and foam fire extinguishers, and hydraulic brakes. Their talents also gave us precast concrete, pressure-sensitive cellophane tape, quick-frozen food, soft contact lenses, zippers, and the Xerox copy machine.[7]

---

4. U.S. Bureau of the Census, *Statistical Abstract of the United States: 1991,* 111th ed. (Washington, DC: U.S. Government Printing Office, 1991), 768.

5. Bureau of Census, *Statistical Abstract,* 744.

6. Ibid.

7. Small Business Administration, *State of Small Business,* 1983 ed., 127, and Karl H. Vesper, *Entrepreneurship and National Policy* (Chicago: Walter E. Heller International Corporation Institute of Small Business, 1983), 40.

PROVIDE SERVICES. Small businesses often do better than big businesses in providing services that require personal contact with customers. When shopping for services such as dry cleaning, hairstyling, portrait photography, travel plans, and auto repairs, customers are often more interested in personal service than in price. Therefore, they are more likely to go to small businesses first.

REPAIR PRODUCTS. Owners of electrical and mechanical products used in homes and businesses depend on entrepreneurs to keep these items working. Think how difficult it would be if refrigerators, microwave ovens, automobiles, and lawn mowers had to be sent back to the factory for repair. Fortunately, this does not have to be done. Automobiles, for example, are kept in running condition by 151,000 repair shops.[8] More than 65,000 shops provide repair for appliances, lawn mowers, microcomputers, and compact disc players.[9]

THE FIELDS OF SMALL BUSINESS

Successful entrepreneurs are in almost every area of American business. The five major fields of business activity are (1) extractive, (2) manufacturing, (3) wholesaling, (4) retailing, and (5) services.

EXTRACTIVE

Extractive enterprises grow products or take raw materials from where they are found in nature. Some of the kinds of enterprises in this field are agriculture, forestry, mining, and commercial fishing.

Examples of extractive enterprises include:

1. Vegetable farms in rural areas surrounding cities
2. Growers of flowers used for special occasions and decorations
3. Sand and gravel companies that provide products for highway and building construction
4. Coal mining for home or industrial fuel
5. Cutting and selling firewood to homeowners who have woodburning stoves and fireplaces

MANUFACTURING

Manufacturing businesses take raw materials and change them into a form that consumers can use. A picture frame manufacturer takes wood and glass and makes a finished product. A baker changes flour, sugar, shortening, and spices into pies and cakes.

Manufacturing, more than any other field, lends itself to big business. This is because it takes large sums of money and many employees to start most of these enterprises. To make automobiles, for

---

8. Bureau of Census, *Statistical Abstract*, 782.
9. Ibid.

example, you need millions of dollars' worth of equipment and materials and hundreds of trained employees.

Opportunities still exist for entrepreneurs in manufacturing. Some examples are printing shops, bakeries, soft-drink bottling plants, machine shops, and meat-packing plants. Also included are ready-mixed concrete plants and cabinet shops. Craftspeople and artisans who make jewelry and furniture are also manufacturers.

Illustration 1-2
Craftspeople like this Alaskan woodcarver are also in the manufacturing business.

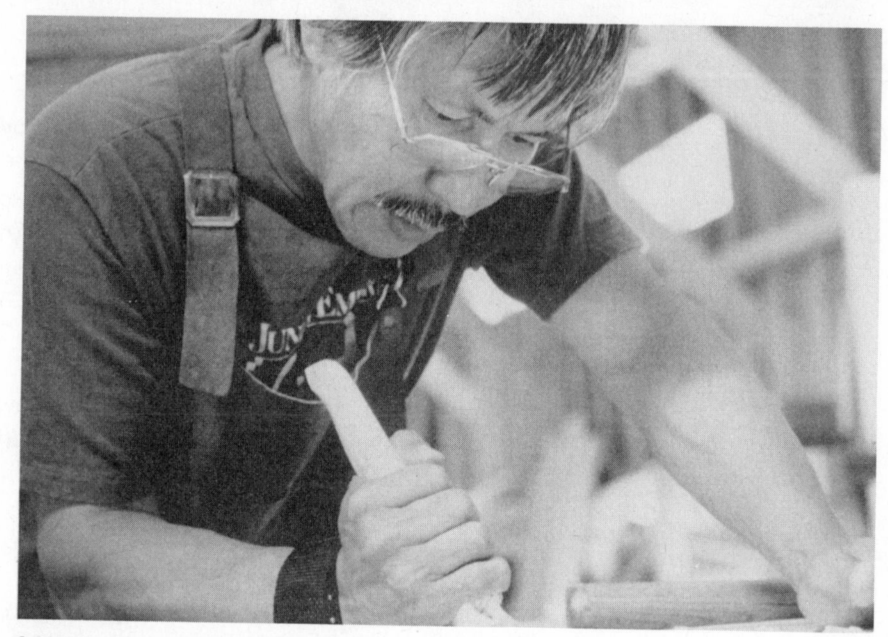

© Alissa Crandall/Alaska Stock Images

WHOLESALING

Wholesalers buy goods from extractive or manufacturing enterprises and sell them to other businesses. They usually buy in large quantities and then sell in small quantities. For example, a maker of garden rakes may sell 3,000 rakes to one wholesaler. The wholesaler, in turn, may sell 60 rakes to each of 50 garden stores. Finally, the stores will sell the rakes one at a time to 60 customers. Many wholesalers are small businesses and have only a few employees.

Some wholesalers specialize in selling goods to institutions such as hotels, hospitals, and schools. Others sell goods that manufacturers use in making other products.

Wholesalers are the usual source of supply for many items sold in retail stores. Examples include hardware, stationery, groceries, fruits, and vegetables. Some provide equipment and supplies for hairstyling salons. Others handle laboratory or office equipment for professionals such as doctors and dentists.

RETAILING

Retailers buy products from wholesalers, manufacturers, or extractive enterprises and sell them to customers. The four forms of retailing are over-the-counter, mail-order, direct, and vending machine retailing.

OVER-THE-COUNTER RETAILING. The most common form of retailing is ***over-the-counter retailing.*** This involves having a store where customers come to shop and buy what they want from the retailer's stock. Examples of small business retailers include clothing stores, shoe stores, building materials stores, auto parts dealers, appliance and television stores, restaurants, antique shops, record shops, and jewelry stores. A number of supermarkets, discount stores, and department stores are owned and operated as small business enterprises.

MAIL-ORDER RETAILING. In ***mail-order retailing,*** customers see the goods they want in catalogs or advertisements. The customers send orders to the retailer's place of business by mail or telephone. After the retailer receives the order, the goods are shipped to the customer. Almost any type of product is sold this way. Small mail-order retailers tend to sell only one type of product. Examples are hobby supplies, gourmet foods and spices, needlework and sewing supplies, and camping equipment. Some of these enterprises offer unique items such as monogrammed handbags or personalized stationery.

DIRECT RETAILING. In ***direct retailing,*** the salesperson goes to the home of the consumer with products or samples. Two types of direct retailing are door-to-door and party plan. In door-to-door selling, the entrepreneur calls on each home in a neighborhood or telephones the customer to set up an appointment to sell products. Cosmetics and household cleaning products are often sold this way. When the party plan is used, one customer hosts a party for several friends. A salesperson comes to the party to display and demonstrate products and to take orders. This plan is used to sell such products as clothing, jewelry, and kitchen items.

Two variations of direct retailing are telemarketing and television home shopping. In telemarketing, a salesperson telephones prospective customers and makes a sales presentation to those who are willing to listen. A few of the products and services sold this way are home and automobile insurance, water softeners, and the services of carpet cleaners and portrait studios. Television home shopping is a retailing innovation developed with the advent of cable TV. Television viewers tuned to a cable shopping channel see a program or show where products are demonstrated by the host or hostess. Consumers may call while the show is on the air to ask questions about the product or to buy it. Purchases are charged to a credit card and shipped directly to consumers.

VENDING MACHINE RETAILING. In ***vending machine retailing,*** the customer deposits money in a machine and receives the goods immediately. A wide variety of products are sold by this method. Soft drinks, candy, and coffee are familiar examples. Other items sold in this manner are cosmetics, small toys, and sandwiches. Vending machines stocked with hot and cold foods and beverages have replaced cafeterias in some offices and factories.

SERVICES

Of all the fields of business, services are generally the easiest to enter. They can usually be started with very little money. Many can be operated from the home or from a small office or shop. Examples are telephone answering, typewriting, word processing, accounting services, bicycle repair, and small appliance repair.

Small enterprises offer hundreds of different kinds of services to consumers, other businesses, and government agencies. Services are found in these categories: (1) personal services, (2) business services, (3) repair services, (4) entertainment and recreation services, and (5) hotel and lodging services.

PERSONAL SERVICES. Enterprises offering personal services perform work directly for a person. Included are hairstyling salons, laundry and dry cleaning establishments, photography studios, travel agencies, funeral homes, day-care centers, baby-sitting services, music teachers, automobile driving instructors, and preparers of income tax forms. There are about 19,000 personal-service enterprises in the United States.[10] Most are small businesses.

BUSINESS SERVICES. Tasks performed by one business firm for another are called business services. Examples include advertising agencies, janitor and building maintenance services, store and building security firms, temporary employee services, and equipment rental businesses. Sign shops, accounting firms, and delivery services are also included in this group.

REPAIR SERVICES. The repair services group includes enterprises that perform work on goods owned by the customer. Examples are businesses that repair automobiles, bicycles, motorcycles, home appliances, and lawn mowers. Also included are upholstery and furniture repair shops, plumbers, electricians, and floor covering installers.

ENTERTAINMENT AND RECREATION SERVICES. Enterprises in the entertainment and recreation services category serve Americans in search of fun and fitness. Examples include bowling alleys, swimming pools, movie theaters, skating rinks, miniature golf courses, water parks, amusement parks, and video movie rental shops.

HOTEL AND LODGING SERVICES. Hotel and lodging enterprises provide lodging for persons on business or pleasure trips. Examples are hotels, motels, trailer parks, guest ranches, recreational camps, and ski resorts.

---

10. Ibid.

INTERNATIONAL BUSINESS

During the 1990s American firms of all sizes have increased their involvement in ***international business,*** the transacting of business and commercial activity across national boundaries. American consumers' demand for foreign-made products combined with foreign consumers' demand for American-made products has stimulated a growing interest in global trade. Because every firm is competing in a global economy, today's entrepreneurs must understand and be able to operate in the world of international business. Small and start-up enterprises may not be affected directly by world trade, but there is a good chance they will be affected indirectly. For example, they may see the prices they pay for imported materials increase or they may lose sales to competing products made in other countries.

Some of the world's largest corporations participate in the international economy by organizing themselves as multinational corporations. A ***multinational corporation*** is a business enterprise that has significant operations in several countries. Its products, financial resources, technology, and management all move across national boundaries. An example of a multinational corporation is the Coca-Cola Company, which manufactures its syrup and concentrate products in forty-four plants worldwide. The company claims 44 percent of the world's soft-drink business and obtains 60 percent of its sales and 80 percent of its profits from operations outside the United States.

Illustration 1-3
Even in Moscow you can order a Coke.

The Coca-Cola Company

Small and start-up enterprises do not operate as multinational corporations. They may, however, participate in international business by exporting, importing, or licensing. ***Exporting*** is the sale and shipping of products manufactured in one country to customers in another country. Exporting is attractive to entrepreneurs who do not have the funds to build manufacturing facilities in other countries. ***Importing,*** the reverse of exporting, involves buying products in another country and bringing them into one's own country. When a company has no immediate plans to make and sell a particular product, it may assign it to another company. Through an arrangement known as ***licensing,*** a foreign firm obtains the rights to make and sell the product in its country and to pay a percentage of each sale to the original company.

THE OUTLOOK FOR ENTREPRENEURSHIP

Through the years, entrepreneurs have turned their ideas into goods and services. In meeting the needs and wants of consumers, they have built rewarding careers for themselves. As you think about having your own enterprise, and being successful as many others have been, you should consider these points: (1) growth of new businesses in the United States, (2) areas of opportunity, (3) causes of business closure, and (4) how to prepare yourself for success.

GROWTH FACTORS

Two forces will affect the growth of new businesses in the coming years. These are a growing population and an increased interest in entrepreneurship.

GROWING POPULATION. The need for goods and services grows with increases in population. The country as a whole is growing, but certain age groups are actually shrinking. The population of the United States exceeded 248 million people in 1990 and could reach 270 million people by 2000.[11] Also, between 1990 and 2000, the number of persons in the 45- to 54-year-old age group is expected to increase by 46 percent. During that same time period it is estimated that the number of 25- to 34-year-olds will decrease by 15 percent.[12] New businesses will be needed, especially enterprises that serve growing population groups.

INTEREST IN ENTREPRENEURSHIP. Never before have so many people been interested in starting their own enterprises. Currently, the average number of new businesses created exceeds 2,000 per day,

11. Ibid., 7, 15–16.
12. Ibid., 536.

up from 250 per day in 1950 and 550 per day in 1965.[13] The level of education has also increased. In comparison with past years, many more people are prepared for entrepreneurship. They have skills that can be sold to others in the form of goods and services. A noticeable trend of the 1990s is that women are joining the ranks of entrepreneurs in increasing numbers. In fact, women are starting new ventures at three times the rate of men.[14]

AREAS OF OPPORTUNITY

The overall outlook for new enterprise is favorable. But certain areas of business have a better chance than others to succeed. Areas with a bright future are (1) services, (2) leisure and recreation, (3) mail order, (4) office supplies and equipment, (5) do-it-yourself products, (6) housing, and (7) home furnishings and appliances.

SERVICES. The demand for services continues to grow rapidly. As more women pursue careers outside the home, more families will depend on service enterprises. Day-care centers and home cleaning services are just two examples. And with higher incomes, many families are buying more home appliances, automobiles, and recreation equipment. This has created a demand for repair services. Some entrepreneurs have become specialized to better serve customers. In addition to general auto repair shops, for example, there are those specializing in brakes, tune-ups, and mufflers. Educational services and business services such as management and tax consulting and public relations are also experiencing growth. Small enterprises will continue to be strong in the service areas because they can give the personal attention consumers want. According to the *Wall Street Journal,* women entrepreneurs have been successful in starting new ventures to serve the demand for services. Over 40 percent of women-owned businesses are service-related.[15]

LEISURE AND RECREATION. Goods and services used in leisure and recreation are expected to be in demand. These include sports clothing, camping goods, boats, and sporting goods. The interest in physical fitness has made sports and recreation clubs popular businesses.

MAIL ORDER. The popularity of mail-order businesses is expected to continue. Ordering goods by mail enables consumers to avoid the shopping problems of traffic and parking. In addition, certain products may be obtained only through mail order. Special cheeses, teas, and spices are examples of items sold through mail-order businesses. Also, parts and accessories for antique and customized automobiles are often sold this way.

---

13. U.S. Small Business Administration, *Handbook of Small Business Data 1988,* 7.

14. Robert D. Hisrich and Michael P. Peters, *Entrepreneurship: Starting, Developing, and Managing a New Enterprise* (Homewood, IL: Richard D. Irwin, 1992), 66.

15. "Small Business, Big Numbers," *Wall Street Journal,* 22 November 1991, sec. R.

OFFICE SUPPLIES AND EQUIPMENT. Whether their sales are up or down, business people need fax machines, calculators, computers, and photocopiers. More entrepreneurs will be selling office supplies and equipment as well as providing repair service.

DO-IT-YOURSELF PRODUCTS. More and more homeowners are paneling walls, laying tile, and pouring concrete themselves. Many, of course, are trying to avoid the cost of paying someone else to do it. Others enjoy these kinds of projects and are doing home repairs as a hobby. Whatever the reason, consumers are buying building materials, supplies, and how-to-do-it books. They are also buying or renting tools and equipment to complete the job.

HOUSING. There will be a continuing need for housing of all types over the next several years. Some entrepreneurs will supply materials used in building houses, apartments, and mobile homes. Carpenters, electricians, and other self-employed persons will actually build and repair the housing units.

HOME FURNISHINGS AND APPLIANCES. Those moving into new homes are likely to need furnishings and appliances. They will be shopping for draperies, microwave ovens, mirrors, lamps, and many other household necessities.

BUSINESS CLOSURES

When an enterprise goes out of business for any reason it is called a ***business closure.*** Most of these are ***voluntary closures;*** that is, the owners close the businesses because they wish to do something else. For example, they may wish to retire, open a different kind of business, or start a company in another location. A business closing its doors and owing money to at least one creditor is known as a ***business failure.*** The chances for an enterprise's survival improve as it grows older. In fact, nearly two out of three businesses that failed in a recent year had been in operation fewer than six years.[16]

Why does a business fail? Some experts say the entrepreneur's lack of management skill is the main cause. Other reasons for failure include the entrepreneur's lack of experience in the particular field of business, insufficient cash to get the business off to a good start, a poor location, or offering a product or service that consumers do not want.

Should the possibility of business failure discourage you from creating your own enterprise? No! However, you should be aware of the risks involved and take steps to avoid as many problems as you can. In other words, you should prepare for success.

---

16. Bureau of Census, *Statistical Abstract,* 25.

PREPARING FOR SUCCESS

Begin preparing for success by learning as much as possible about your chosen field of business. You can do this by taking classes in school and by working in a business similar to the one you intend to start.

Your school may offer classes directly related to your future enterprise. For example, you may be able to study auto repair, general merchandise retailing, interior design, or printing to prepare for business ownership in those fields. In addition, classes in accounting, marketing, recordkeeping, keyboarding, and computer programming are useful to entrepreneurs.

Through work experience, you will come in contact with many of the problems faced by entrepreneurs in your chosen field. The variety of the tasks is usually more important than the length of your work experience. Thus, you should learn all the major activities, such as making the product, providing the service, keeping records, or selling. You can obtain work experience by enrolling in a cooperative education program or by working after school and in the summer. After graduation, you may choose to work full-time for someone else until you obtain the necessary skills.

Illustration 1-4
Accounting skills are useful to entrepreneurs.

One of the best ways to prepare for success is to know yourself. It may seem surprising, but thousands of people start enterprises each year without thinking of what it is like to be self-employed. They know what some of the advantages are, but they have given little or no thought to the disadvantages. In other words, they really do not know if entrepreneurship is for them.

Once you have decided to create a new enterprise, you should start preparing a business plan. A business plan is a written description of every part of a new enterprise. Beginning with a definition of the business you intend to conduct, a business plan maps out the course for the enterprise. While you will refine this definition as you develop each part of the business plan, it is important to have at least an initial definition that answers the key question: What will you offer customers, and why?

An airline pilot would not think of flying from coast to coast without a flight plan. An entrepreneur should not think of starting a new enterprise without a business plan. In this text-workbook, you will learn how to prepare a business plan in which you will

1. Define the business you intend to conduct.
2. Describe your qualifications for becoming an entrepreneur.
3. Explain the benefits you will offer to customers.
4. Analyze the competition.
5. Set goals for the enterprise; for example, how much profit you will make each year.
6. Answer questions about money for starting the enterprise such as: How much money do you need? Where will you get the money? What is the interest rate?

Does entrepreneurship fit into your career plans?

ACTION STEPS FOR ASPIRING ENTREPRENEURS

Follow these action steps to help you prepare for a career as an entrepreneur:

1. List as many reasons as you can why you should consider entrepreneurship as a career.
2. Describe the personal qualities that you believe helped Sam Walton become a successful entrepreneur.
3. Identify those qualities that you and Sam Walton have in common.
4. Go to the library to find out more about one of the entrepreneurs (e.g., Frederick W. Smith, Steven P. Jobs, or Edwin Land) mentioned in this chapter.
5. Try to answer this question when thinking about your future and your career: Do I want to work for myself or for someone else?

BUILDING YOUR ENTERPRISE VOCABULARY

Match the following terms with the statements that best describe applications of those terms. Write the letter of your choice in the space provided.

a. entrepreneur
b. services
c. managing
d. multinational corporation
e. extractive enterprises
f. manufacturing businesses
g. wholesalers
h. retailers
i. voluntary closures
j. small business

_______ 1. Preparing the daily work schedule and making sure the monthly sales report is completed.
_______ 2. "I like being an independent business owner."
_______ 3. Using wood, nails, and glue to make kitchen cabinets.
_______ 4. Working for yourself instead of for someone else.
_______ 5. Buying a dozen or more of each new compact disc release and selling them one at a time to customers.
_______ 6. Farms and mines are examples.
_______ 7. You cannot touch them, but you still pay for them.
_______ 8. A business buys a truckload of lighting fixtures and sells them in smaller quantities to hardware stores.
_______ 9. Coca-Cola operates more than forty plants worldwide.
_______ 10. The owners decided to go out of business so they could retire.

UNDERSTANDING KEY CONCEPTS

Write a short answer to each of the following questions.

1. What three key features do most new enterprises have in common?

____

____

____

____

2. What is the difference between entrepreneurship and small business management?

____

____

____

____

3. List three reasons why the study of entrepreneurship may be important to you.

____

____

____

4. List the important roles performed by small businesses.

____

____

____

____

____

5. Name the five major fields of business activity.

____

____

____

____

6. What are the forms of retailing?

____

____

____

7. Why must entrepreneurs understand international business?

____

____

____

____

____

8. What factors will affect the growth of new businesses in the coming years?

____

____

____

9. Why do service enterprises tend to be small businesses?

____

____

____

10. Describe the two types of business closure.

____

____

____

____

11. What are the reasons for business failure?

____

____

____

____

12. What are the six steps in developing a business plan?

____

____

____

____

____

____

APPLYING YOUR ENTERPRISE KNOWLEDGE

These activities will give you a chance to apply what you have learned in Chapter 1.

1. List the names of two businesses, in your community or elsewhere, involved in each of the five fields of business activity. Then list the kinds of goods or services sold by each.

Field of Business	Name of Firm	Goods or Services Sold
Extractive	1. 2.	
Manufacturing	1. 2.	
Wholesaling	1. 2.	
Retailing	1. 2.	
Services	1. 2.	

2. Assume that your next-door neighbors are interested in starting a small business. They ask you to suggest two areas of business that have a better chance than others to succeed. How would you answer? Write your answers in the space provided below and at the top of page 21. For each of your choices, give first the name of the area of business and then the reasons why it is a promising field to enter at this time.

3. List ten products or services that you and others in your age group buy often. Place a check mark (✓) in front of each one that you purchase from a small enterprise.

____

____

____

____

____

____

____

____

____

____

SOLVING BUSINESS PROBLEMS: LAWN GROOMERS

Mike and Don decided they could earn some extra money by starting a lawn-mowing business. Since both plan to be entrepreneurs, they thought the experience gained in establishing and operating Lawn Groomers, a lawn-mowing business, would be valuable in their future careers. This business required a minimum of equipment, most of which they already had and knew how to operate. In addition, Mike and Don were able to work outdoors for as many, or as few, hours as they wanted.

Lawn Groomers was in operation from May to October, the season for lawns. Mike and Don did most of the work themselves. They hired temporary employees when they had more work than the two of them could handle.

As partners in the venture, Mike and Don agreed on most aspects of running the business. The major area of disagreement was what additional services, if any, they should offer to customers and how much they should charge for those services. Mike said, "We're in the business of mowing lawns. We'll trim around trees, sidewalks, and next to fences, because that's a part of the total job of cutting the grass. As far as I'm concerned, Lawn Groomers should not perform any other services. We should do one thing, and do it well."

Don thought for a moment and then said, "Sure, we're in the lawn-mowing business. What if a customer asks us to remove a tree stump from the yard, spread fertilizer on the lawn, or prune the shrubs and trees? I believe we should perform the service if the customer asks. Maybe we should even do some of this work free of charge. It doesn't take long to fertilize a lawn, and customers may like it so much they would never consider using another lawn service. Of course, the customers would provide the fertilizer. I'll go so far as to say that we should be ready and willing to perform any job related to a lawn. Lawn mowing is only a part of it."

1. What is the major problem in this case?

____

____

____

2. What alternatives do Mike and Don have for solving the problem?

____

____

____

____

____

3. Of the alternatives you identified, which one do you recommend? Why?

____

____

____

____

____

4. What will be the consequences if Mike and Don ignore your recommendation?

____

____

____

BUSINESS PLAN PROJECT

In the "Business Plan Project" section at the end of each chapter, you will find learning activities to aid you in creating a new enterprise. As you study each chapter, you should ask yourself: How would this information apply to me if I decide to become an entrepreneur?

When you have finished the "Business Plan Project" sections for all eight chapters, you will have a complete business plan for a new enterprise of your choice.

The purpose of this first part of the business plan project is to help you start thinking about entrepreneurship. From the facts given in this chapter, complete the following assignment:

> Assume that you wish to go into business for yourself. Select the field of business you would like to enter; that is, extractive, manufacturing, wholesaling, retailing, or services. Then state the reasons why you selected this field. Write your answer in the space provided on this page and page 24.

My choice for a field of business: ____________________

Reasons for my choice: ____________________

CHAPTER 2

EXAMINING ENTREPRENEURSHIP AS A CAREER

Entrepreneurs organize, manage, and assume responsibility for new enterprises. Their goal is to earn a profit by providing products and services everyone needs. If entrepreneurs are successful in carrying out this task, they can build rewarding careers for themselves.

Many opportunities exist to start new enterprises. But before you decide to become an entrepreneur, you should find out what is involved. This chapter examines entrepreneurship as a career. You will see if, and how, entrepreneurship fits into your future.

Learning Objectives

After you have studied Chapter 2, you should be able to:

1. Discuss the advantages and disadvantages of working for yourself.
2. Describe eight types of entrepreneurs.
3. Identify the characteristics common to successful entrepreneurs.
4. Estimate your personal financial needs.
5. Compare and contrast the three major ways of going into business for yourself.
6. Explain why an entrepreneur may want to consider a sideline or a home-based business.

ENTREPRENEUR PROFILE Sandra Kurtzig

As Sandra Kurtzig tells the story: "In 1971 I was a twenty-four-year-old working wife thinking about starting a family, not a business. But things didn't turn out quite the way I'd planned." Sandra Kurtzig was looking for a job she could do at home. Using her knowledge of computer programming, her experience selling computer time-sharing, and $2,000, she started ASK Computer Systems, Inc., in a spare bedroom. Her husband Arie's first initial, A, and her initials, SK, were combined to form the company name. The selling of the company's stock to the public for the first time in 1981 made Sandra the chief executive officer (CEO) of the largest public company founded and run by a woman.

Sandra was born into a family of entrepreneurs. Her father operated a small candy store for a few years and then started designing and building homes and apartment houses, first in Illinois and then in California. Her mother decorated the homes and handled the advertising, sales, and rental activities. As a child growing up, Sandra did not see either of her parents work regular nine-to-five hours. Instead, she saw two people who worked hard for long hours, but who enjoyed what they were doing. Sandra also realized the value of work and, while in high school, was a sales clerk in the linens department at Bullock's department store.

Meeting a challenge has always been important to Sandra. She is also inspired to take action when she is told she is not capable of accomplishing something. When she was in elementary school, her parents were told that she had an average IQ. Sandra did not like being labeled as average. She responded by working as hard as she could and concentrating on doing what she liked. She enjoyed math and chemistry courses because the problems had clear-cut answers; she preferred to stay away from English and social studies. When teachers told her she was not eligible for admission into an advanced math class, she set out to prove them wrong. She studied the text, completed all the assignments, and passed a test to gain entry into the class. She ended up with the highest grade in the class.

At age 20, Sandra earned a bachelor's degree from the University of California-Los Angeles, where she was a math major and a chemistry minor. Immediately enrolling at Stanford University, she received a master's degree in aeronautical engineering one year later. Her first job out of college was with IBM, for whom she worked one day and quit. Her second job was in sales with Virtual Computing, a new time-sharing company. While she had had several lucrative job offers, she chose Virtual Computing because the idea of a new company with growth potential appealed to her. This job ended three months later when she refused to sign a non-compete agreement which would have kept her from taking a job with any competitive company for two years after leaving this firm.

Sandra's next job, which was in sales with GE Computer Time-Sharing, lasted about three years. By this time she was 24 years old and her next job was in her own business, ASK Computer Systems, Inc., which would become a major computer software company.

ASK's software helps manufacturers run inventory, accounting, purchasing, and other operations. In the firm's early days, Sandra spent most of her time writing computer programs. As the business grew, new employees were hired to write the programs, freeing Sandra to concentrate on other tasks. She found that her strengths were her ability to sell, communicate, hire good people, look for new opportunities, and guide ASK's overall operations.

Sales revenues grew from $50,000 for the first full year, which ended in 1972, to $8,300,000 in 1980. By 1982 ASK was the eighth-fastest-growing public company in the country and the nation's fastest-growing software company. In 1985, when sales were $79,000,000, Sandra stepped down from active management as CEO of the company to raise her two sons. She felt she could always go back into the business world, but she could never relive her sons' childhood years.

By 1989, ASK was no longer considered the industry leader. Further, the price of its stock had dropped. Concerned about the future of the company, the board of directors asked Sandra to return as CEO. Believing that her sons were now old enough so that she could again play an active role in the business, in September 1989 Sandra returned to lead the company she had founded eighteen years earlier. By the early 1990s, ASK's sales were over $400 million per year.

Source: Sandra L. Kurtzig with Tom Parker, CEO: Building a $400 Million Company from the Ground Up *(New York: W. W. Norton, 1991), and Maria Shao, "Sandra Kurtzig,"* Business Week *(April 5, 1991): 72.*

WORKING FOR YOURSELF COMPARED TO WORKING FOR OTHERS

Thousands of Americans are interested in starting their own business. However, many think only of the rewards and give little thought to the risks. In this section, you will look at both the advantages and the disadvantages of being an entrepreneur.

ADVANTAGES OF WORKING FOR YOURSELF

Those who choose entrepreneurship as a career usually do so for five appealing reasons: (1) personal satisfaction, (2) independence, (3) profit, (4) job security, and (5) status.

PERSONAL SATISFACTION. To some persons, the chief reward of working for yourself is personal satisfaction. ***Personal satisfaction*** means doing what you want with your life. As an entrepreneur, you will be able to spend each workday in a job you enjoy. For example, if you like photography, you may start your own studio. Each time a customer is pleased with a portrait, you will receive personal satisfaction.

You may also gain personal satisfaction from aiding the community in which you live. Entrepreneurs supply goods and services and create jobs for residents. They also buy goods and services from other local enterprises, borrow money from local banks, and pay taxes.

INDEPENDENCE. Another advantage of entrepreneurship is independence. ***Independence*** is freedom from the control of others. As an entrepreneur, you decide how you will use your knowledge, skills, and abilities. Compared to those who work for others, entrepreneurs have more freedom of action. They are in charge and can make decisions without first getting the approval of someone else.

If you choose to become an entrepreneur, you can develop any creative ideas you have—assuming, of course, that the business is legal and that you have the money to invest.

PROFIT. One of the major rewards expected when starting a new business is profit. ***Profit*** is the amount of sales income left after all expenses have been paid. Profits go to the owner of a business. Being self-employed, you would receive all the profits. Very often, increased time and effort put into the enterprise result in increased income. This is not often the case when you work for someone else.

JOB SECURITY. Many enterprises are created by persons who are seeking job security not available elsewhere. ***Job security*** is the assurance of continuing employment and income. Entrepreneurs cannot be laid off, fired, or transferred to another city, nor can they be forced to retire at a certain age because of company policy.

STATUS. Self-employed people often enjoy personal benefits, such as status. ***Status*** is a person's social rank or position. Entrepreneurs receive attention and recognition through customer contact and public exposure. As a result, they may enjoy status above that of many blue-collar and white-collar workers.

Closely related to social status is pride in ownership. Most people enjoy, at least for a while, seeing their names on buildings, on stationery and business cards, and in advertisements.

Illustration 2-1
Most people are proud to see their family name on a product.

DISADVANTAGES OF WORKING FOR YOURSELF

In addition to knowing the advantages of working for yourself, you should also be aware of the disadvantages: (1) possible loss of invested capital, (2) uncertain or low income, (3) long hours, and (4) routine chores.

POSSIBLE LOSS OF INVESTED CAPITAL. A risk of entrepreneurship is the possibility of losing invested capital. ***Invested capital*** refers to the entrepreneur's money used in starting the enterprise. As a general rule, the riskier the business, the greater the profit potential. If the enterprise succeeds, profits may be high; if not, invested capital may be lost. The entrepreneur risks losing personal and family savings. It may take years to repay banks, suppliers, or individuals who made loans to get the business started.

UNCERTAIN OR LOW INCOME. Another disadvantage of owning your own business is the possibility of uncertain or low income. Unlike paychecks of salaried workers, profits usually vary from month to month. This is true even in well-established enterprises. When income is available, there may not be enough to meet personal and family needs. This is often the case during the first six to twelve months of operation. The level of sales and income tends to be low in these early months when the business is not known to many people.

LONG HOURS. Entrepreneurs do not punch time clocks, and they are not forty-hour-a-week workers. In a survey reported in the *Wall Street Journal,* 79 percent of the entrepreneurs said they worked more than forty hours in an average week.[1] Many entrepreneurs work fourteen or fifteen hours a day, six or seven days a week. The owner is often the first to arrive in the morning and the last to leave at night. Business hours are set at the convenience of customers, not the desire of the owner. For example, many shopping center stores are open from 9 A.M. to 9 P.M. Likewise, many restaurants open before noon and do not close until after midnight. Manufacturers and building contractors may have to work overtime to meet customer deadlines. Not only are the hours long, but also the time between vacations. Twenty-two percent of those in the *Wall Street Journal* report said they do not take vacations; 18 percent take one week of vacation each year.[2] Some entrepreneurs feel they cannot leave their businesses for more than one or two days at a time.

ROUTINE CHORES. Running your own business may involve chores you do not like. For example, though new business owners expect to do some paperwork, many do not realize how much is required until the business is started. By that time, some feel they are buried under a mound of paper. One of the surprises is the extent of recordkeeping for items such as billing, payroll, and taxes. Maintenance and cleaning are other chores that must be performed each day. While it is possible to hire employees to perform these routine duties, a shortage of cash may prevent owners from doing so.

IDENTIFYING TYPES AND CHARACTERISTICS OF ENTREPRENEURS

An entrepreneur is a person who attempts to earn a profit by taking the risk of operating a business enterprise. While all entrepreneurs may have certain characteristics in common, no two entrepreneurs are exactly alike.

1. John B. Hinge, "Small Business, Big Numbers," *Wall Street Journal,* 22 November 1991, sec. R.

2. Ibid.

TYPES OF ENTREPRENEURS

Entrepreneurial characteristics combined in different people result in different types of entrepreneurs. Karl Vesper has classified entrepreneurs into the following types: (1) solo self-employed individuals, (2) team builders, (3) independent innovators, (4) pattern multipliers, (5) economy-of-large-scale exploiters, (6) capital aggregators, (7) acquirers, and (8) buy-sell artists.[3]

SOLO SELF-EMPLOYED INDIVIDUALS. Entrepreneurs who work alone or with only a few employees are known as ***solo self-employed individuals.*** They generally perform the work themselves rather than assigning it to other people. Solo self-employed individuals are perhaps the most numerous of all entrepreneurs. Their ranks include small store and repair shop owners, independent sales representatives, attorneys, and physicians.

TEAM BUILDERS. Entrepreneurs who expand small, usually one-person businesses into larger companies are ***team builders.*** An example is the self-employed electrician who gradually hires additional employees until a full-scale electrical contracting firm is established. Many of the nation's largest companies started out this way. For example, in 1927, J. Willard Marriott started a nine-stool root beer stand. Over the years, his root beer stand was built into a corporation that operates hotels and restaurants throughout the world and accounts for annual sales of more than $7 billion.[4]

INDEPENDENT INNOVATORS. Individuals who create companies to manufacture and sell products they have invented are ***independent innovators.*** Examples are An Wang and Edwin Land. Wang's invention of the magnetic-pulse controlling device for computer memory led to the creation of Wang Laboratories, Inc., a manufacturer of computers and word processing equipment. Land founded the Polaroid Corporation on the success of one of his inventions, the world's first polarizing sheet material.

PATTERN MULTIPLIERS. Entrepreneurs who build several units of an effective business are known as ***pattern multipliers.*** The entrepreneurs may have designed and built the original business, or they may have purchased a business started by someone else. To illustrate, the first McDonald's fast-food restaurant was opened in 1948 by brothers Dick and Maurice McDonald. Ray Kroc was impressed with this hamburger operation and, in 1954, he became their national franchise agent and sold franchises to other people. In 1961, Kroc bought out

---

3. Adapted from Karl H. Vesper, *New Venture Strategies,* rev. ed. (Englewood Cliffs, NJ: Prentice-Hall, 1990), 3-8.

4. Gary Hoover, Alta Campbell, and Patrick J. Spain, eds., *Hoover's Handbook of American Business 1992* (Austin, TX: The Reference Press, 1991), 355.

the McDonald brothers for $2.7 million. Ray Kroc established himself as a pattern multiplier by building a number of units patterned on the proven business format developed by the McDonald brothers.[5]

ECONOMY-OF-LARGE-SCALE EXPLOITERS. When a firm has lower average costs due to its large sales volume, economies of large scale are involved. Entrepreneurs who can sell a large volume of goods at reduced prices are ***economy-of-large-scale exploiters.*** Discount store operators are one example of this type of entrepreneur. Because of the larger scale of their establishments, they may be able to afford advanced and specialized equipment such as the scanners built into the checkout counters at some larger supermarkets. This equipment enables one cashier to handle more customers in less time, thus lowering the store's payroll expense because fewer cashiers are needed. Economy-of-large-scale exploiters often obtain merchandise at price discounts because they buy in such large quantities. An example of this type of entrepreneur is seasoned discount retailer Sol Price. Price, with his son Robert, Rick Libenson, and Giles Bateman, opened the first Price Club warehouse in San Diego in 1976.[6] Today, the company operates sixty-seven of its warehouse-style stores in nine states and three Canadian provinces. Customers pay a membership fee each year and spend in excess of $125 on a typical visit. This figure is well above the average amount spent at most other general merchandise stores. The average sales volume for each Price Club store is just short of $100 million per year.

CAPITAL AGGREGATORS. Entrepreneurs who take the lead in pulling together the large amounts of capital needed to start enterprises in the financial industry are ***capital aggregators.*** At the age of 28, William Donaldson joined Dan Lufkin and Richard H. Jenrette to found Donaldson, Lufkin & Jenrette, Inc., a Wall Street investment banking firm that gained the reputation of being innovative.[7] One of the services provided in return for a fee by this type of firm is to sell new stock issued by corporations. Proceeds from the sale of new stock go directly to the corporation. Other examples of capital aggregators are those who use their capital-raising skills to help start banks, mutual funds, and insurance companies.

ACQUIRERS. People who become entrepreneurs by buying an existing business are ***acquirers.*** Entrepreneurs lacking work experience in particular fields have successfully entered those fields by acquiring businesses already in operation. (Both the advantages and disadvantages of buying an existing business are discussed later in this chapter.)

---

5. Kenneth Morris, Marc Robinson, and Richard Kroll, *American Dreams: One Hundred Years of Business Ideas and Innovation from The Wall Street Journal* (New York: Lightbulb Press, 1990), 156-57.
6. Hoover, Campbell, and Spain, *Hoover's Handbook of American Business 1992*, 444.
7. Gary Weiss, "William Donaldson," *Business Week* (April 5, 1991):78.

Finding a business that someone is ready to sell is usually not difficult; however, determining the value of the business, or whether it is even worth buying, is a more difficult task. Check the classified section of your local newspaper. You may be surprised at the number and variety of businesses for sale in your community.

BUY-SELL ARTISTS. Rather than making their money from the day-to-day operations of a business, ***buy-sell artists*** turn a profit by buying a business and then selling it at a higher price. Buy-sell artists usually buy companies with problems that they solve before they sell the company. Typical actions include reducing costs and payrolls and eliminating unprofitable products. In most cases, buy-sell artists do not wish to own a particular company for more than a few years.

Illustration 2-2
Some entrepreneurs specialize in buying existing businesses.

CHARACTERISTICS OF SUCCESSFUL ENTREPRENEURS

Whatever the type of entrepreneur, successful entrepreneurs are often described as being persons who (1) take moderate risks, (2) have self-confidence, (3) work hard, (4) set goals, (5) are responsible, (6) are innovative,[8] (7) have technical knowledge, and (8) have business knowledge.

MODERATE IN TAKING RISKS. Persons who quit secure jobs and invest money in a new enterprise have much at stake. They are taking a risk. Their businesses may succeed and provide profits for years to come. On the other hand, the business may fail and cause financial ruin. Entrepreneurs are willing to take middle-of-the-road or moderate

8. Items 1 through 6 adapted from Nicholas C. Siropolis, *Small Business Management: A Guide to Entrepreneurship,* 2d ed. (Boston: Houghton Mifflin Co., 1982), 33-36, and David C. McClelland, *The Achieving Society* (Princeton, NJ: D. Van Nostrand Co., 1961), 207, 222.

risks. ***Moderate risk*** means the chances of winning are neither too small nor too great. That is, results are not left purely to chance, nor are they sure to happen. Instead, they depend on a person's abilities and actions.

Entrepreneurs like challenges suited to their skills. They want to make things happen rather than let them happen by chance.

SELF-CONFIDENT. Successful entrepreneurs have self-confidence. ***Self-confidence*** means believing you can achieve what you set out to do. You are not afraid to take chances. You know you can get the job done. This strong inner feeling about oneself is important for the owner of a small business. It can often spell the difference between success and failure. Self-confidence sustains the owner during difficult times in the growth of the new business.

Having self-confidence also means you are realistic and you know the limits of your abilities. You know what you can and cannot do. Entrepreneurs are not afraid to ask for help with difficult tasks.

HARD-WORKING. Creating a new enterprise is hard work. Helping customers, keeping accounting records, and cleaning are just a few duties you may have to perform on a given day. You may also have to make deliveries, order supplies, and repair equipment. Much work must be done with few, if any, employees to help. Therefore, good health and physical stamina are important.

Only when their businesses are firmly established do entrepreneurs feel the freedom to put in fewer hours. Even then, however, they are ready to work when a job must be done.

GOAL-ORIENTED. Do you know what you want to achieve in life? Successful entrepreneurs know where they are going by setting goals. A ***goal*** is an objective, something you plan to achieve. Your chances of becoming a business owner are slim unless you first decide you want to own your own business.

An example of a goal could be to get a summer job in a restaurant. Another example could be to have your own restaurant within five years.

You should learn to focus on one goal at a time. Direct all your energy toward this goal. When you have attained it, go to the next goal. If you try to pursue several goals at once, you can become confused and lose sight of your target.

RESPONSIBLE. When you are ***responsible,*** you answer or account for what happens. You accept blame for failure, and you accept credit for success. As an entrepreneur, you will be responsible for the success or failure of your business. You will set goals and hold only yourself responsible if they are not met.

Entrepreneurs have many responsibilities. They must pay debts and wages. They must keep promises to employees or customers. They must also be willing to make personal sacrifices. For example, during busy seasons, the owner may not be able to take vacations with the family.

INNOVATIVE. Successful entrepreneurs are ***innovative*** because they introduce new ideas or methods. They try to improve existing products and services or create new products and services. Entrepreneurs invented fiberglass snow skis, video games, ballpoint pens, zippers, and automatic transmissions. They also introduced fast-food restaurants, quick oil-change shops, and computer stores.

Perhaps you have a new idea for a gift shop, a landscaping service, or a day-care center. Of course, not all ideas can be turned into profitable businesses. If you find one that can, you may build a satisfying career for yourself.

KNOWLEDGEABLE ABOUT TECHNICAL FACTORS. You must have technical knowledge to succeed as an entrepreneur. ***Technical knowledge*** is what you know about a product or service. For example, a photographer must know how cameras operate. A pet shop owner must learn about the care of animals. A printer must have knowledge of different printing processes and papers.

One way to gain technical knowledge is by taking classes in school. Examples would be classes in repairing cars, preparing foods, growing plants, or typewriting. You may also gain technical knowledge from a hobby or from a job in your area of interest. Make sure you have technical knowledge before you start a new enterprise.

KNOWLEDGEABLE ABOUT BUSINESS FACTORS. You will also need business knowledge. ***Business knowledge*** is knowing how to operate the enterprise. Entrepreneurs must see that all tasks are performed appropriately. Examples are helping customers, setting prices for products and services, paying bills, planning advertising, and keeping accounting records.

ESTIMATING YOUR PERSONAL FINANCIAL NEEDS

It may be months or even years before the enterprise can provide you with enough money for living expenses. Every year, promising new enterprises are closed before they really get a chance to prove themselves. The owners simply run out of money and must obtain salaried jobs to support themselves and their families.

It is important, therefore, to estimate your personal financial needs. Do this for a period of three to six months. Then make sure you will have the money to cover that time period. If the money will not be available, you would be wise to delay the starting of the enterprise. Figure 2-1 is a list of expense items you may wish to include in your personal budget.

SELECTING A WAY OF GOING INTO BUSINESS

The aspiring entrepreneur who possesses the necessary personal characteristics, skills, and money can select one of three different ways of going into business: (1) buying an existing business, (2) starting a business from scratch, and (3) buying a franchise.

Figure 2-1
Personal Budget Items

Rent or mortgage payment on home
Insurance (life, home, health, auto)
Real estate taxes
Payments on debts (loans, charge cards, etc.)
Charitable or church contributions
Utilities (water, gas, electricity, telephone)
Medical and dental (office visits, prescriptions, etc.)
Groceries
Meals away from home
Clothing
Car operation and repair
Recreation (movies, etc.)
School costs
Personal (e.g., hairstyling salons, gifts)
Laundry and dry cleaning
Club dues
Baby-sitting or day-care services

BUYING AN EXISTING BUSINESS

You may be interested in buying an ***existing business*** because the business is already set up. At first glance, buying an existing business may appear to be a way to avoid many of the beginner's hazards. The risks, however, are never totally eliminated. Anyone with enough money to pay the purchase price can buy a business; the question is whether that person will be able to operate the business successfully. Therefore, an individual must examine the advantages and disadvantages of buying an existing business before making a purchase decision.

ADVANTAGES OF BUYING AN EXISTING BUSINESS. Buying an existing business may have these advantages: (1) a proven record, (2) established clientele, (3) established location, (4) bank and supplier relationships, (5) trained employees, (6) established facilities, and (7) a low purchase price.

Proven Record. A business has a ***proven record*** when it has earned a profit for the current owner. Records are available to show what sales, expenses, and profits the new owner may expect.

Established Clientele. When buying an existing business, you normally get an ***established clientele.*** This is a group of regular customers who are in the habit of buying goods and services from the enterprise. A business with an established clientele has a group of customers who think favorably of the business, and the new owner will probably be able to count on their continuing support.

Established Location. Buying an existing business saves time and money in finding a location. A major problem in starting a new business is finding the right location. An existing business has already shown the value of its location if it is successful.

Bank and Supplier Relationships. A local banker may be familiar with the enterprise because of dealings with the former owner. This relationship could be helpful to a new owner who needs a business loan. Also, purchase arrangements with suppliers may be continued by the new owner. Seeking out dependable suppliers of equipment, materials, and services can be a time-consuming process.

Trained Employees. With the business, the buyer may acquire reliable employees. Getting employees who know the products, services, and customers is an advantage. Otherwise, the entrepreneur must hire and train employees, taking time and attention away from other aspects of the business.

Established Facilities. When you buy an existing enterprise, you are ready to do business. Equipment and display fixtures are already installed. Signs are in place, and the parking lot is paved. If it is a gift shop, merchandise is displayed in windows and stocked on shelves. If it is a carpenter's shop, woodworking equipment is anchored in place and ready to use. There may even be a supply of wood on hand.

Low Purchase Price. An owner who is eager to sell a business may give you a favorable buy. Your purchase price may be less than the current cost of buildings, equipment, and inventory. Of course, you should make sure you are actually getting a bargain.

DISADVANTAGES OF BUYING AN EXISTING BUSINESS. You may not want to buy an existing business because of these disadvantages: (1) a poor record, (2) ill will, (3) wrong location, and (4) poor physical condition.

Poor Record. Why does the current owner want to sell? The current owner may have health problems, retirement plans, or the desire to pursue other business interests. On the other hand, the owner may want to get out of the enterprise because it has a record of losing, or because problems are expected in the future. For example, new competition may be coming into the area, or a highway that now brings customers to the business may be relocated.

Ill Will. The previous owner may have treated customers and business persons poorly. Such treatment causes ***ill will,*** which is a feeling of hostility, toward the business. A bad reputation is a major disadvantage. If you should buy the existing business, you would have to draw customers back to the business. You would also have to develop positive relationships with bankers and suppliers. In short, you would have to change a poor image into a favorable one. This is not an impossible task, but it may be just as easy to start a new business from scratch.

Wrong Location. What was once a good location may no longer be convenient for customers. The enterprise may be too far from other business or shopping facilities. Other problems may include lack of parking space and traffic congestion.

Poor Physical Condition. Be prepared to spend some money to improve the physical condition of the business. You may have to remodel buildings or repair or replace equipment. You may have a problem of energy usage. Many older buildings are not insulated properly, causing high bills for heating and cooling. Delivery trucks that come with the business may not get good gas mileage. You should also check items in inventory. In a clothing store, for example, some items of apparel may be soiled or torn. In a plumbing shop, pieces of pipe and fittings may be rusty and of little value.

STARTING A BUSINESS FROM SCRATCH

Starting from scratch means you will do all the work of establishing the enterprise. Before you choose this way of going into business, you should look at the advantages and disadvantages.

ADVANTAGES OF STARTING A BUSINESS FROM SCRATCH.

The advantages of starting a business from scratch are (1) freedom to make decisions, (2) opportunity to develop image, (3) choice of location, and (4) choice of physical facilities.

Freedom to Make Decisions. When you start an enterprise, you are free to make your own decisions. You choose when and how to get started. You are not limited to a certain location or to specific products or services. You hire your own employees and choose suppliers you want to use. In other words, you decide everything.

Opportunity to Develop Image. How customers feel about doing business with an enterprise is its ***image.*** Some enterprises enjoy a favorable image and others do not. In a new business, you can develop a favorable image from the start.

Choice of Location. Deciding where to locate is one of the most important decisions you will make. It can mean the difference between

Illustration 2-3
Choice of location is a very important business decision.

success and failure. Of course, you will be limited by the amount of money available to buy or rent facilities. But you will probably be able to select from several possible locations. Starting a new business is a way to obtain the best location.

Choice of Physical Facilities. Deciding on location is closely related to deciding on physical facilities. ***Physical facilities*** refer to buildings and parking lots or driveways. When starting from scratch, you will be able to choose the physical facilities you need. You can either shop around until you find the right ones, or you can have them built. You will then be assured of having the right amount of space in the layout you desire.

DISADVANTAGES OF STARTING A BUSINESS FROM SCRATCH.

Some of the disadvantages of starting from scratch are: (1) no record, (2) no established clientele, (3) time-consuming tasks, and (4) difficulty in obtaining a loan.

No Record. Whereas an existing business has a proven record, the new business has no record. The best you can do is estimate what sales, expenses, and profits will be.

No Established Clientele. Brand-new businesses do not have an established clientele. As an entrepreneur, you would have to spend a lot of time attracting customers. You hope the customers you do get will develop a habit of buying from you. Even so, sales volumes build slowly. Weeks or months may pass before you are able to draw even a small salary.

Time-consuming Tasks. It takes time to launch an enterprise. You will have to search for the right location. Then you will have to install machines, display cases, or other needed items. You have to order goods. When they are received, you must store or display them. Another time-consuming task is hiring and training new employees.

Difficulty in Obtaining a Loan. Many new entrepreneurs underestimate the amount of money they will need. They spend all their money in getting the enterprise started. Then they have trouble getting a loan to keep the business going. Banks usually prefer to lend to established businesses.

BUYING A FRANCHISE

Thousands of Americans have become entrepreneurs by buying franchises. A ***franchise*** is a legal agreement or contract between a company and an entrepreneur. The company, called the ***franchisor,*** is a manufacturer, wholesaler, or service company. The entrepreneur, called the ***franchisee,*** is permitted to sell the franchisor's goods or services in a certain area. The franchisee pays fees to the franchisor. In return, the franchisor grants use of the company name and gives help to start the business. As shown in Figure 2-2, many different kinds of franchised businesses exist in the United States.

Several franchise names have become household words. Midas Muffler, Holiday Inn, McDonald's, Hertz car rentals, Kampgrounds of America, Century 21 Real Estate, and H & R Block tax service are franchise names known from coast to coast.

Figure 2-2
Franchising in the United States

Kinds of Franchised Businesses	Number of Establishments
Auto and truck dealers	27,600
Restaurants	102,100
Gasoline service stations	111,700
Retailing (nonfood)	54,100
Auto and truck rental services	10,600
Automotive products and services	38,600
Business aids and services	67,300
Construction, home improvement, maintenance, and cleaning	28,300
Convenience stores	17,500
Educational products and services	13,300
Equipment rental services	3,400
Food retailing	25,400
Hotels, motels, and campgrounds	11,100
Laundry and dry cleaning services	2,600
Recreation, entertainment, and travel	10,300
Soft drink bottlers	800
Miscellaneous	8,400
Total number of establishments	533,100

Source: U.S. Bureau of the Census, Statistical Abstract of the United States: 1991, *111th ed. (Washington, DC: U.S. Government Printing Office, 1991), 778.*

ADVANTAGES OF BUYING A FRANCHISE. When you buy a franchise, you buy the right to do business under a certain name. This does not include a building, equipment, or inventory. The franchisee purchases these items separately. Advantages of franchising are (1) initial training, (2) financial assistance, (3) established brand name or image, (4) proven method of doing business, and (5) continuing assistance.

Initial Training. Management training provided by the franchisor helps to make up for the entrepreneur's lack of experience. The training covers a broad range of topics useful in getting the enterprise started. Examples are accounting, advertising, purchasing, and supervision of employees.

Financial Assistance. Financial assistance offered to franchisees can take several forms. Some franchisors lend money for the purchase of supplies and equipment. Others provide guidance on obtaining loans through banks. With the help of a successful franchisor, the entrepreneur is often able to obtain more favorable credit terms.

Established Brand Name or Image. In a well-known franchise system, the franchisee does not have to work to establish a reputation. Customers are already familiar with the goods or services offered. Advertising by the franchisor may keep the product or service name in front of the public.

Proven Method of Doing Business. Franchisees have the benefit of proven methods of doing business. The methods and practices used in the business have been developed and tested through a process of trial and error. Operating manuals are developed. Thus, entrepreneurs learn from the franchisor's experience and avoid many mistakes.

Continuing Assistance. Even after the business is established, franchisors may continue to provide assistance. They may help in controlling expenses and inventory or give advice on expanding the building or adding new products.

DISADVANTAGES OF BUYING A FRANCHISE. Entrepreneurs should also consider these disadvantages of franchising: (1) limited control, (2) franchise fees, and (3) image problems.

Limited Control. As a franchisee, you may have only ***limited control.*** A franchisee cannot make some decisions without prior approval of the franchisor. You will use the franchisor's name for the business, and you will only be able to sell certain products or services. Many franchises must remain open during specified hours and days. After investing your own money, you may still feel as though you are working for someone else.

Franchise Fees. A franchisee must pay two types of fees to the franchisor. One is the ***initial fee,*** or down payment, which the franchisee pays when the franchise is purchased. The other is a ***royalty,*** which the franchisee pays continually for the life of the franchise. For example, a franchisee may pay 5 percent of gross sales each month to the franchisor. Some franchisees are also required to spend a certain percentage of each sales dollar on advertising.

Image Problems. If other franchisees mistreat customers and harm the image of the franchise, you could be hurt. Your sales and profits may suffer because of the actions of others.

EVALUATION OF A FRANCHISE. Before buying a franchise, be sure to study it closely for your own protection. This study should include an evaluation of (1) the franchisor, (2) the product or service, (3) the franchise contract, (4) the potential customers, and (5) you—the franchisee.[9]

---

9. Wendell O. Metcalf for the U.S. Business Administration, *Starting and Managing a Small Business of Your Own,* 3d ed., The Starting and Managing Series, Vol. 1 (Washington, DC: U.S. Government Printing Office, 1973), 48.

The Franchisor. When trying to decide if a franchise is right for you, one of the key questions you should seek to answer is: What can the franchise do for me that I cannot do for myself? Learn as much as possible about the franchisor. For example, find out how long the company has been in business and what kind of reputation it has. Visit franchises that are already in operation and discuss the franchise and relations with the franchisor. Be cautious of such meetings that the franchisor arranges. You may not get a clear picture of the business. For example, the person you talk to may be one of the few successful franchisees; or people may be working together in promoting dishonest schemes.

The Product or Service. What is the future for the product or service the franchise offers? Will consumers be buying more, the same amount as today, or less five years from now? Keep in mind that consumers' needs and wants change often. What appears to be a favorable franchise today may not be one in a few years.

The Franchise Contract. The relationship between the franchisor and the franchisee is described in the franchise agreement or contract. This is usually a complex and lengthy document. Before signing the contract, make sure you understand all the terms. For example, does the contract specify the amount of the initial fee and the way royalty fees are determined? Does the contract cover all aspects of the franchise?

The Potential Customers. A franchise will not succeed unless there are enough customers in the market area where it is located. Therefore, you should determine the population in your area. Will it increase, remain the same, or decrease in the next five years? You should also consider your competition. Will there be other entrepreneurs selling the same products and services in the immediate area?

You—the Franchisee. As the final step in evaluating a franchise, you should look at yourself as a franchisee. This should include an evaluation of your ability and your attitude toward all aspects of the franchise. Do you know where you will get the money for the initial fee? How does the cost compare to that of buying an existing business or starting from scratch? Perhaps the most important question is: Are you willing to trade your independence for the advantages the franchise offers?

SIDELINE AND HOME-BASED BUSINESSES

Entrepreneurs who wish to get into business on a smaller scale can do so through either a sideline business or a home-based business. A ***sideline business*** is started after regular work hours or on weekends during other employment. A ***home-based business*** is an enterprise operated in or from the home that produces goods or services. It may be a full-time or a part-time enterprise.

A sideline business could also be a home-based business. Electricians, plumbers, and painters who work from their homes as well as graphic artists, consultants, and accountants who work in their homes are all examples of home-based businesses. Many enterprises started as small sideline or home-based businesses remain small. Others, however, grow to become leaders in their industries. Sandra Kurtzig, for example, started ASK Computer Systems, Inc., in a spare bedroom. When the business outgrew that space, it was moved out of her home into a commercial location. Today, the company's sales exceed $400 million per year.

The size or scale of the business at start-up can be crucial to its survival. It is one thing to plan a new business; it is quite another to execute the plan. Assume you have prepared a business plan describing your business, your qualifications, and the benefits you will offer to customers. In fact, you have accounted for every significant detail and answered every question, except for one: Do you have the money called for in the plan? You have some funds available, but not enough to start the venture as planned. What do you do?

Chances for new-business success are significantly reduced when you do not have the funds available to support the business and your personal living expenses. Rather than not starting the business, you could revise the business plan and start the venture on a smaller scale than originally planned. For example, instead of quitting your full-time job to start a mail-order gift business, you could start and run the business from your home on the side. As additional funds become available, you could increase the size gradually. You might offer just a few items in the beginning when you have little money to invest in inventory. As dollars from initial sales flow in and you can afford to increase the size of the inventory, you could offer a wider selection of gifts to your customers.

Illustration 2-4
Operating a business from the home is often a good way to start.

D.P. Valenti/H. Armstrong Roberts

ACTION STEPS FOR ASPIRING ENTREPRENEURS

Follow these action steps to help you prepare for a career as an entrepreneur:

1. Identify the two advantages and the two disadvantages of working for yourself that are most important to you.
2. Select the type of entrepreneur (solo self-employed, independent innovator, etc.) that you think is the most interesting and explain why.
3. Describe how you will pay your personal living expenses while you are starting a business.
4. Explain why the hazards of getting into business are not eliminated completely when buying an existing business.

BUILDING YOUR ENTERPRISE VOCABULARY

Match the following terms with the statements that best describe applications of those terms. Write the letter of your choice in the space provided.

a. profit
b. status
c. independent innovators
d. pattern multipliers
e. moderate risk
f. responsible
g. established clientele
h. franchise
i. royalty
j. sideline business

_______ 1. Each month a franchise owner pays an amount equal to 6 percent of sales to the franchisor.
_______ 2. A scientist started a company to make and sell the product he invented.
_______ 3. After expenses were paid, about ten cents of each dollar from sales remained.
_______ 4. "The lack of sales is my fault. I underestimated the competition."
_______ 5. Developing and selling specialized computer software when not working at your full-time job at the newspaper.
_______ 6. Being recognized by many people as the owner of a successful local business.
_______ 7. The right to sell a manufacturer's cars and trucks in the area.
_______ 8. Opening five automobile tune-up shops and trying to duplicate the success of your first one.
_______ 9. "My family and I have been shopping here for twenty years."
_______ 10. Enough of a challenge to make the business interesting.

UNDERSTANDING KEY CONCEPTS

Write a short answer to each of the following questions.

1. What are the advantages and disadvantages of working for yourself?

ADVANTAGES

____

____

____

____

DISADVANTAGES

____

____

____

____

2. Name eight types of entrepreneurs.

3. List the characteristics of successful entrepreneurs.

4. What are the five factors you should study before getting into franchising?

5. What alternatives do you have if you lack the funds to start the enterprise as described in your business plan?

6. Compare the three ways of going into business by writing the advantages and disadvantages of each in the space provided.

Ways of Going into Business	Advantages	Disadvantages
Buying an Existing Business		
Starting a Business from Scratch		
Buying a Franchise		

APPLYING YOUR ENTERPRISE KNOWLEDGE

These activities will give you a chance to apply what you have learned in Chapter 2.

1. Are you the kind of person who can get a business started and make it go? Answers to the following questions should help you decide. Under each question, check the answer that says what you feel or comes closest to it. Be honest with yourself.

Are you a self-starter?

❑ I do things on my own. Nobody has to tell me to get going.
❑ If someone gets me started, I keep going all right.
❑ Easy does it; I don't put myself out until I have to.

How do you feel about other people?

❑ I like people. I can get along with just about anybody.
❑ I have plenty of friends—I don't need anyone else.
❑ Most people irritate me.

Can you lead others?

❑ I can get most people to go along when I start something.
❑ I can give the orders if someone tells me what we should do.
❑ I let someone else get things moving. Then I go along if I feel like it.

Can you take responsibility?

❑ I like to take charge of things and see them through.
❑ I'll take over if I have to, but I'd rather let someone else be responsible.
❑ There's always some eager person around wanting to show how smart he/she is. I say let him/her.

How good an organizer are you?

❑ I like to have a plan before I start. I'm usually the one to get things lined up when others want to do something.
❑ I do all right unless things get too goofed up. Then I quit.
❑ You get all set and then something comes along and presents too many problems. So I just take things as they come.

How good a worker are you?

❑ I can keep going as long as I need to. I don't mind working hard for something I want.
❑ I'll work hard for a while, but when I've had enough, that's it!
❑ I can't see that hard work gets you anywhere.

Can you make decisions?

❑ I can make up my mind in a hurry if I have to. It usually turns out fine.
❑ I can if I have plenty of time. If I have to make up my mind fast, I think later I should have decided the other way.
❑ I don't like to be the one who has to decide things.

Can people trust what you say?

❑ You bet they can. I don't say things I don't mean.
❑ I try to be on the level most of the time, but sometimes I just say what's easiest.
❑ Why bother if the other person doesn't know the difference?

Can you stick with it?

❑ If I make up my mind to do something, I don't let *anything* stop me.

❑ I usually finish what I start—if it doesn't get fouled up.
❑ If it doesn't work right away, I quit. Why beat your brains out?

How good is your health?
❑ I *never* run down!
❑ I have enough energy for most things I want to do.
❑ I run out of energy sooner than most of my friends seem to.

Now count the checks you made.

How many checks are there beside the first answer to each question? ______
How many checks are there beside the second answer to each question? ______
How many checks are there beside the third answer to each question? ______

If you placed most of your checks beside the first answers, you probably have a lot in common with successful entrepreneurs and may have what it takes to start and run a business. If not, you may be able to succeed with the help of a partner, preferably one with strengths to counterbalance your weaknesses. If you chose the third answers most frequently, you are probably not suited for entrepreneurship.

Source: Adapted from U.S. Small Business Administration, Checklist for Going into Business, *Management Aids no. 2.016 (Washington, DC: U.S. Government Printing Office, 1982), 2-3.*

2. Give the names of three franchised businesses in your community. Name the types of goods or services sold and describe the image of the franchises.

FRANCHISE BUSINESS #1

Name: ____________________

Goods or services sold: ____________________

____

Image: ____________________

____

____

FRANCHISE BUSINESS #2

Name: ____________________

Goods or services sold: ____________________

____

Image: ____________________

____

FRANCHISE BUSINESS #3

Name: ____

Goods or services sold: ____

____

Image: ____

____

____

____

3. In an interview with an entrepreneur in your community, ask the following questions.

   a. Why did you decide to go into business for yourself?

   ____

   ____

   ____

   ____

   ____

   b. What technical and business knowledge did you have prior to starting the enterprise?

   ____

   ____

   ____

   ____

   c. What problems did you face when trying to start the enterprise?

   ____

   ____

   ____

   ____

   d. How many hours do you work each week?

   ____

4. In the space provided below, estimate the personal financial needs for a family consisting of a mother, father, and two children, ages 3 and 6.

PERSONAL FINANCIAL NEEDS FOR THREE MONTHS

Expenses	Amount
Rent or mortgage payment on home	$ ________
Insurance (life, home, health, auto)	________
Real estate taxes	________
Payments on debts (loans, charge cards, etc.)	________
Charitable or church contributions	________
Utilities (water, gas, electricity, telephone)	________
Medical and dental (office visits, prescriptions, etc.)	________
Groceries	________
Meals away from home	________
Clothing	________
Car operation and repair	________
Recreation (movies, etc.)	________
School costs	________
Personal (e.g., hairstyling salons, gifts)	________
Laundry and dry cleaning	________
Club dues	________
Baby-sitting or day-care services	________
Other expenses	________
TOTAL PERSONAL EXPENSES FOR THREE MONTHS	$ ________

SOLVING BUSINESS PROBLEMS: OLD DEPOT RESTAURANT

Twenty years ago, when the railroad company decided to close the depot near the edge of town, Carolyn and John Miles leased the property. They remodeled the building and opened their new business, the Old Depot Restaurant. The menu consisted of luncheon specials, dinners, and an assortment of desserts.

Carolyn and John's ideas about the type of restaurant that would be successful in town must have been correct. The Old Depot Restaurant has been both popular in town and profitable to the Miles family.

Within the last few years, the dessert items on Old Depot's menu have gained a reputation of their own. A dessert cart is brought to the table when patrons have finished the main course. Rarely is the waiter or waitress told, "I don't care for dessert." Many people buy a whole pie or cake to take home with them. Even those who have eaten dinner at home or in another restaurant will have their dessert at the Old Depot.

Katherine Miles, Carolyn and John's daughter, is now managing the restaurant. In studying the various items on the menu, she found that desserts are the highest profit items. Following a discussion with her parents, she has decided to package dessert items, particularly pies and cakes, and distribute them for sale through supermarkets in the area. The brand name that has been chosen is "Old Depot Dessert Cart."

The business, which will be reorganized and called Miles Foods Company, will consist of two divisions: Old Depot Restaurant Division and Old Depot Dessert Cart Division. Katherine will be president of Miles Foods and will continue to manage the restaurant. She is in the process of hiring a manager for the dessert division. Several people applied for the job by sending their personal data sheets to Katherine. She has narrowed the choice to two people: Ralph Adams and Michelle Wilson. However, Katherine is having trouble making the final selection. Both Ralph and Michelle appear to be qualified for the job, and they each made good impressions in their interviews. When she asked them to describe briefly how they would operate the dessert division, Ralph answered, "As the manager, I would oversee the day-to-day operations of the business." Michelle said, "I would run the dessert division just as an entrepreneur would."

1. Which of the two people should Katherine hire? Why?

____

____

____

____

____

____

____

____

____

2. Would a person who has the characteristics of an entrepreneur be happy working for someone else?

3. Assume that Katherine wants to hire Michelle, but Michelle will accept the job only if she is allowed, in most cases, to run the business as an entrepreneur. Is there anything Katherine could do that would satisfy Michelle's request? Explain.

BUSINESS PLAN PROJECT

After you have written the information required on pages 53 and 54, you will have a personal data sheet to include in your business plan.

PERSONAL DATA SHEET

Name: ______________________________

Address: ______________________________

Telephone: ______________________________

SCHOOLS ATTENDED

Name and Location of School	Years Attended	Major Area of Study

RELEVANT SUBJECTS STUDIED IN SCHOOL

____

____

____

SCHOOL ACTIVITIES, HOBBIES, OR INTERESTS

____

____

____

WORK EXPERIENCE

Employer name: ______________________________

Address: ______________________________

Supervisor: ______________________________

Telephone: ______________________________ Dates of employment: ______________

Duties: ______________________________

Employer name: ______________________________

Address: ______________________________

Supervisor: ______________________________

Telephone: ______________________________ Dates of employment: ______________

Duties: ______________________________

Employer name: ______________________________

Address: ______________________________

Supervisor: ______________________________

Telephone: ______________________________ Dates of employment: ______________

Duties: ______________________________

REFERENCES

Name: ______________________________

Title: ______________________________

Address: ______________________________

____

Telephone: ______________________________

Name: ______________________________

Title: ______________________________

Address: ______________________________

____

Telephone: ______________________________

Name: ______________________________

Title: ______________________________

Address: ______________________________

____

Telephone: ______________________________

CHAPTER 3

USING YOUR CREATIVITY

Creativity is the ability to visualize and implement new ideas. Some of these ideas are "new things to do"; others are "new ways of doing things." The new things include the many products and services introduced into the marketplace every day. The new ways of doing things are various methods, procedures, and processes that help businesses operate more efficiently. Both types of ideas are essential to the growth and development of any business. This chapter discusses sources of new enterprise ideas, methods of generating ideas for new enterprises, and the application of creativity to business operations.

Learning Objectives

After you have studied Chapter 3, you should be able to:

1. Describe sources of new enterprise ideas.
2. Explain methods of generating new enterprise ideas.
3. Discuss how creativity can be used to find ideas that will make businesses run more efficiently.

ENTREPRENEUR PROFILE Ray Kroc

Ray Kroc developed McDonald's Corporation into the world's largest food service organization and, as a result, he earned a place in business history and established himself as the kind of entrepreneur called a pattern multiplier. (Pattern multipliers are discussed in Chapter 2.)

Ray was born in 1902 in Chicago, Illinois. His father worked for Western Union and his mother ran a neat, well-organized house. His mother's example may have been the basis for his insisting that every restaurant in the company must, above all else, be neat and well organized.

While he was growing up, Ray always had odd jobs to earn spending money. As a teenager as well as in later years, he earned extra money playing the piano. Ray was a thinker and a dreamer. He looked for ways to apply his creativity. Ray did not consider his dreaming a waste of energy because his dreams were linked to action. For example, while in high school, Ray dreamed up the idea of starting a music store; it was not long before the store was open for business. He and two of his friends each invested a hundred dollars to launch the venture. Ray earned his part of the investment by working at the soda fountain in his uncle's drugstore. Even though the music store was open for only a few months, Ray demonstrated that he preferred to take action rather than just talking about an idea.

Ray Kroc spent more than thirty-two years of his adult life selling paper cups, milkshake mixers, and other products to the food service industry. He learned what successful salespeople believe are valuable skills: the ability to see things as customers see them and a knack for meeting customers' needs and interests rather than your own. People who develop these skills see new trends as they develop in the marketplace.

Ray heard about a busy restaurant operated by Dick and Maurice McDonald in San Bernardino, California. The McDonald brothers developed the Speedee Service System restaurant concept featuring a red and white tile building with Golden Arches and the little Speedee logo. Ray was told that the small restaurant was so busy during lunchtime that all eight milkshake machines were running continuously. Realizing that each machine was capable of making five shakes at a time, Ray decided to travel to San Bernardino. He had to see for himself how a single hamburger stand with no inside seating could do so much business.

Ray found that soon after the stand opened at 11 A.M., the parking lot was full and customers were marching up to the windows and back to their cars with bags full of hamburgers, french fries, and milkshakes. Impressed by what he saw, Ray knew immediately that he wanted to get into this business. The McDonald brothers began issuing franchises and the first franchised unit was opened in Phoenix, Arizona, on May 15, 1953. By the time they met Ray Kroc, the McDonald brothers had issued fourteen franchises. In 1954, Ray became their national franchise agent and sold franchises to other people. He was not responsible for operating these restaurants.

On April 15, 1955, Ray opened his first restaurant in Des Plaines, Illinois. This unit served as a model where prospective franchisees could see the operation in action. By the end of 1957, there were forty restaurants in the McDonald's System. All of the restaurants were franchised until 1959, when some units were "company-owned." When Ray bought out the McDonald brothers in 1961 for 2.7 million there were 331 restaurants in the McDonald's System. Ray continued to insist on the qualities upon which McDonald's reputation was built: courtesy, cleanliness, service, value, and product quality consistency.

Ray never stopped working for McDonald's. He used a little go-cart to zip around in for a couple of years before his death in 1984. In his last year, and while in a wheelchair, he went to the office nearly every day and served as senior chairman of the company. As of December 1992, the company had nearly 13,000 restaurants in sixty-five countries and a total annual sales volume in excess of $19 billion.

Source: Ray Kroc, Grinding It Out: The Making of McDonald's *(New York: St. Martin's Press, 1977); John F. Love,* McDonald's: Behind the Arches *(New York: Bantam Books, 1986); and Helen Farrell, Manager, McDonald's Archives.*

SOURCES OF NEW ENTERPRISE IDEAS

If you want to be an entrepreneur, you should be alert at all times for new or more efficient ways to meet the needs and wants of customers. These ideas can come from many sources, and they can appear at any time. Some people find ideas for new enterprises while reading newspapers or magazines. Others discover ideas while they are pursuing a hobby or when they are attending a merchandise show or a craft and hobby show.

NEWSPAPERS

A convenient way to begin the search for new enterprise ideas is to read your local newspaper. When reading, pay attention to the classified advertising section. ***Classified advertising*** (often called want ads) consists of advertising messages grouped together in one part of the newspaper under headings such as Help Wanted, Autos for Sale, Business Opportunities, and Business Services. The most helpful headings when looking for enterprise ideas are Business Opportunities and Business Services.

BUSINESS OPPORTUNITIES. People wanting to sell their businesses often advertise them in the business opportunities section of classified advertisements. ***Business opportunity advertisements*** usually describe the enterprise to be sold, the location, and sometimes the selling price. One way to become an entrepreneur is to buy an existing business. Therefore, you should know what businesses are for sale in your community.

Business opportunity advertisements can be important to you for other reasons. For example, if you have decided to study entrepreneurship opportunities in a particular industry, the ads can help you select a specific type of enterprise.

Assume you are interested in opening a food service establishment. By reading advertisements, you can get a good idea of the variety of enterprises available in the food service industry. Once you are aware of what is available, you can determine if any match your interests or abilities.

If your career plans are uncertain, business opportunity advertisements can offer a lot of clues to what your interests are.

BUSINESS SERVICES. Persons with specialized business or technical skills to sell reach potential customers through ***business services advertisements.*** In these ads, it is the service that is for sale, not the enterprise providing the service.

Business services advertisements can be helpful as you think about your future. You may have taken a bookkeeping or accounting course at one time because you thought about working in a bank or in another local business. Did you realize that you could also use these skills in your own enterprise? Business services advertisements have helped many people become aware of new career paths.

NEWSPAPER ARTICLES. Entrepreneurs must be alert to the world around them, and they can stay informed by reading newspapers regularly. Ideas for new enterprises are found frequently in newspaper articles. Look for articles describing new types of businesses. For example, a recent story proclaimed, "Messenger services thrive as businesses seek to send items quickly across town." This story may give someone the idea to start a local messenger service. Perhaps the enterprise would offer pickup and delivery service of small parcels, medical records, and legal documents.

If you are going to start a new business enterprise, you may want to concentrate your efforts on products or services with large sales potential. Some have been described in newspapers as follows:

- Older Americans demand nutritional foods. By the end of the century, 25 percent of the people will be in this age group.
- Business is brisk for those who repair VCRs and telephones.
- No-frills warehouse stores are successful despite breaking conventional retailing rules.
- We're eating $2.5 billion in cookies each year.
- Many companies are renting, rather than buying, office furniture.

Such newspaper reports may inspire someone to become an entrepreneur to sell one or more of the products or services having large sales potential.

Pay attention to news items that signal changes in consumer needs. Such changes often mean that consumers will buy either more or less of certain products or services. For example, you may read that there is more interest in physical fitness. Therefore, look for new enterprise ideas that are related to physical fitness, such as selling sporting goods or health foods. Other examples are health spas and organic farming.

Illustration 3-1
Working parents are a growing market for in-home child care.

An aspiring entrepreneur might read about the increase in the number of employed parents. The prospective entrepreneur might decide to open a day-care center or to offer in-home child care on a contract basis.

MAGAZINES

Special-interest magazines and trade publications have other ideas for new enterprises.

SPECIAL-INTEREST MAGAZINES. Articles and advertisements in specific areas of interest appear in ***special-interest magazines.*** An article in a camping magazine may prompt you to ask, "Why isn't there a camping supplies store in my town?" Your pursuit of an answer to the question may be the starting point for a new enterprise. Likewise, you may get the idea to rebuild and sell used dirt bikes from reading a motorcycle magazine. A list of special-interest magazines is shown in Figure 3-1.

Figure 3-1
Special-Interest Magazines

Area of Interest	Magazine
Antiques	*American Collector's Journal* *Antique Market Report* *Antique Monthly*
Camping and Outdoor Recreation	*Backpacker* *Canoe* *Field & Stream*
Cars	*Car and Driver* *Cars & Parts Magazine* *Hot Rod Magazine*
Computers	*Byte* *Compute!* *Computer Entertainment* *Creative Computing*
Crafts and Hobbies	*Ceramics Monthly* *Crafts Magazine* *Miniature Collector*
Electronic Communication	*Video Times* *Home Satellite TV* *Hands-on Electronics*
Home Gardening	*Flower & Garden* *Garden Design* *Horticulture, The Magazine of American Gardening*
Motorcycles	*Cycle World* *Dirt Bike* *Motor Cyclist*
Sports	*Bicycling* *Runner's World* *Tennis*

To find special-interest magazines you like, check with relatives, friends, and the school and public libraries. Many special-interest magazines are sold by subscription and on newsstands and magazine racks in stores.

TRADE PUBLICATIONS. Magazines and newspapers designed for people working within a particular business or field are known as ***trade publications.*** They contain helpful information regarding new products or services likely to become popular soon. You will find information in the articles as well as the advertisements. Trade publications are available in many libraries. You may want to read one or more of those listed in Figure 3-2.

Figure 3-2
Trade Publications

Area of Interest	Magazine
Advanced Technology	*Printed Circuit Fabrication* *Robotics Today* *Semiconductor International*
Agriculture	*Farm Chemicals* *Animal Health & Nutrition* *Grain Age*
Automotive	*Autobody and the Reconditioned Car* *Automotive Body Repair News* *Automotive Rebuilder*
Building and Construction	*Fence Industry* *Interior Construction* *Remodeling Contractor*
Fashion and Clothing	*Apparel World* *Apparel Merchandising* *Women's Wear Daily*
Florists	*Florist* *Flower News* *Greenhouse Grower*
Hairstyling Salons	*Beauty School World* *Modern Salon* *Salon Talk*
Hotels, Motels, Restaurants	*Hotel and Resort Industry* *Lodging Hospitality* *Restaurant Business*
Interior Design	*Design Today* *Interiors* *The Designer*
Landscape and Garden Supplies	*Landscape & Irrigation* *Lawn Care Industry* *Yard and Garden*

Figure 3-2 *(continued)*

Area of Interest	Magazine
Manufacturing	*Industrial Equipment News* *Metal Finishing* *Wood & Wood Products*
Office Management	*Data Management* *Modern Office Technology* *Words*
Printing	*Graphic Arts Monthly* *Package Printing* *Quick Printing*
Retailing	*Chain Store Age* *Discount Store News* *Progressive Grocer* *Merchandising*
Sporting Goods	*Archery Business* *Golf Business* *Ski Business*

HOBBIES

Hobbies are activities you pursue for pleasure and relaxation. They are often the source of ideas for new enterprises. For example, if you enjoy buying and selling antiques and other collectibles, you may be able to expand your hobby into a profitable full-time enterprise. A business related to your hobby will enable you to spend more time doing what you enjoy most.

MERCHANDISE SHOWS

Another way to find ideas for new enterprises is to attend merchandise shows sponsored by manufacturers and distributors. Two types of merchandise shows are public and trade. Each serves a different purpose.

PUBLIC SHOWS. Places where manufacturers and distributors display and demonstrate their products to the public are called ***public shows.*** They are open to all persons who wish to attend. An admission fee may be charged in some cases, and shows may last several days. Public shows are often held in fairgrounds buildings, convention centers, or sports arenas. Watch for newspaper advertisements about public shows.

Examples of public shows that are popular in many parts of the country include the following:

- *Home and Garden Shows.* Home improvements, appliances, remodeling, and gardening products and services are featured.
- *Sports, Vacation, and Travel Shows.* Boats, camping equipment, and sporting goods are exhibited. Colorful displays are also set up by states, resort areas, and hunting and fishing lodges.

- *Camping and Recreational Vehicle Shows.* These shows feature tent campers, truck campers, vans, and motor homes.
- *Auto Shows.* Domestic and imported cars are displayed.

When you go to a public show, you will see salespersons and product demonstrators who will answer your questions. Leaflets and brochures describing products are usually available.

By visiting a public show, you may discover an enterprise idea that matches your interests and abilities. For example, at a home and garden show you may see exhibits of those appliances and building materials that are gaining in popularity. If you are skilled in home remodeling, these products may form the basis of an idea for a new enterprise.

TRADE SHOWS. Exhibits of products from many suppliers organized by groups of manufacturers or wholesalers are known as ***trade shows,*** and they are open only to people engaged in a particular line of business or trade. For example, apparel shows are held each year so retailers can preview new fashions and order merchandise in time for the next season. Salespeople are on hand not only to accept orders and set up delivery dates but also to discuss changes in styles and fashions. Shows are also held in trade areas such as furniture, hardware, housewares, sporting goods, books, medical supplies, jewelry, computers, and office equipment.

These shows can be sources of new enterprise ideas. After attending a show of computer equipment, for example, you might decide to look for entrepreneurship opportunities in that field because of its growth potential. Perhaps you will decide to sell microcomputers and software.

You must realize that trade shows are not held everywhere. They are most frequently found in the larger cities. Remember that admittance to trade shows is limited to members of the trade and that there may be an admission fee. If you would like to attend a show and are not working in the trade, a friend in the appropriate trade area may take you as a guest.

CRAFT AND HOBBY SHOWS

Craft and hobby shows are places where people show others what they make or study in their spare time. For example, coin collectors may display their collections for all to see. Those who work with pottery may demonstrate the craft for others.

You may get ideas for new enterprises by observing activities at craft and hobby shows. For example, you may notice that amateur photographers shop often for supplies and equipment to use in their hobby. Perhaps you will decide to start a business to sell those items.

You usually do not have to look too far to find a craft or hobby show. They are held frequently in local shopping malls, convention centers, exhibit halls, or parks. Be alert for newspaper announcements that tell the place, date, and time for a show in your area. You should also be prepared to pay a small admission fee at some of these shows. What craft and hobby shows are held in your community?

Illustration 3-2
An African drum maker demonstrates his product at a folk art festival.

© W. Marc Bernsau/The Image Works

METHODS OF GENERATING NEW ENTERPRISE IDEAS

Some new enterprise ideas are found by chance. Most, however, come from the entrepreneur's conscious efforts. You can generate ideas for new enterprises by conducting surveys, brainstorming, making observations, and keeping a notebook of ideas.

CONDUCTING SURVEYS

One way to stimulate ideas for new enterprises is to find out what consumers need and want. You can obtain this information from surveys. A ***survey*** involves asking a number of people a series of questions and then summarizing their answers. Surveys can be either informal or formal.

INFORMAL SURVEYS. You can conduct an ***informal survey*** by talking to your family and friends. You may ask them what new businesses they think are needed in town, or you may ask if there are products or services they are not able to purchase locally. Another way to get some information is to ask: If you were to start your own business, what would it be? What products or services would you offer? Why? Answers to these questions may give you new enterprise ideas to think about.

When you observe business activity in the community, you are conducting an informal survey. Observation might reveal the need for particular enterprises. Perhaps there is no bicycle repair shop in town, and there appear to be many bicyclists in the area. Maybe you have noticed that a catering service is needed for parties. If you live near a tourist or resort area, you may be able to sell items made by local artisans.

FORMAL SURVEYS. A ***formal survey*** involves either interviewing many people or asking them to complete a questionnaire. Contact persons from throughout the community, especially those who are potential customers for the new enterprise. Formal surveys are useful in identifying shortcomings or weaknesses in existing enterprises and in determining needed products or services.

Shortcomings in Existing Enterprises. The existence of several businesses of one type does not necessarily mean you should not start a similar enterprise. For example, consumers may not be satisfied with the existing carpet cleaning services in a town. However, they may continue to patronize these businesses simply because there are no other choices. A carpet cleaner who can please customers may not have to worry about competition.

The more people you interview, the better your chances of getting a clear picture of businesses in the community. Using a form like the one in Figure 3-3 can be helpful in your survey.

Figure 3-3
Survey to Determine Shortcomings in Existing Enterprises

Please answer these questions about carpet cleaning services in this community.

1. What type of residence do you have?

______ house ______ mobile home

______ apartment ______ other ______________

2. Have you ever had your carpet cleaned by a carpet cleaning service?

______ No Why not?______________________
Thank you for answering these questions.
______ Yes (End of interview)

3. For each pair of phrases (e.g., worked fast–worked slowly), circle the phrase that best describes the personnel and the service.
The carpet cleaning personnel:

were courteous	were not courteous
worked fast	worked slowly
came as scheduled	did not come on schedule
took care in moving furniture	were careless in moving furniture
were skilled in their jobs	were not skilled in their jobs

The service itself was:

worth the price	not worth the price

Thank you for answering these questions.

Needed Products or Services. Formal surveys of businesses in a community may reveal new enterprise opportunities. Retailers, wholesalers, and manufacturers could be asked what products or services they purchase in other cities. For example, businesses may have to buy wooden shipping crates or office supplies from dealers in another city because they are not available from local sources. Making needed products or services available locally can be the basis for a new enterprise.

After you have identified needed products or services, you should answer these questions:

1. Am I interested in starting an enterprise to provide these products or services?
2. Do I have the skills and financial resources required to start this enterprise?

Perhaps you would like to make picture frames and sell them to retail stores. To get as much information about the picture frame business as possible, you may decide to conduct a formal survey. The survey form shown in Figure 3-4 on page 66 could be used to gather information from department stores or gift shops.

BRAINSTORMING

Another method of generating ideas for new enterprises is brainstorming. ***Brainstorming*** is a technique used to solve a problem by generating as many ideas as possible. You may use brainstorming in a group or by yourself.

As you search for new enterprise ideas, you will probably brainstorm by yourself. However, you may be able to do this more effectively if you first learn how this technique works in a group.

You can get practice in brainstorming by getting together with two or three people. One person should be the leader and another the recorder. The recorder's job is to list the ideas as they are stated. Compile the ideas on a chalkboard or on a large sheet of paper that everyone can see.

Illustration 3-3
All ideas–even wild ones–are welcomed in brainstorming sessions.

Figure 3-4
Survey to Determine Needed Products or Services

I am interested in starting a new business in this town. Would you please answer these questions about the picture frames you sell.

1. Which type of picture frame is your best seller? Second? Third?

   a. ______________________

   b. ______________________

   c. ______________________

2. What is the price for each of your three best-selling picture frames?

   a. $ ______________________

   b. $ ______________________

   c. $ ______________________

3. What are your three slowest-selling styles?

   a. ______________________

   b. ______________________

   c. ______________________

4. Please indicate which styles are purchased directly from the manufacturer and which ones are purchased from a wholesaler:

From manufacturer	**From wholesaler**
______________________	______________________
______________________	______________________
______________________	______________________
______________________	______________________

5. Which manufacturers and wholesalers are located in this town or in a nearby town?

   ____

   ____

   ____

6. Would you prefer to buy from a local manufacturer of picture frames?

   ______ Yes

   ______ No Why? ______________________

7. Describe briefly the service you expect from a manufacturer.

   ____

   ____

8. What is your approximate annual sales volume in picture frames?

   $ ______________________

Brainstorming begins with a question from the leader. Someone in the group suggests an answer, then everyone else changes it or adds to it. Each idea leads to one or more other ideas. The result is a chain reaction of ideas.

In addition to getting the session started, the leader must keep it going. The leader should be ready to add an idea when others run out of ideas. This often restarts the process.

Follow these rules in the brainstorming group:[1]

1. *Don't criticize another person's ideas.* Group members will tend to talk less if this happens. This means fewer ideas will be expressed. Group leaders should discourage such phrases as: "That's a dumb idea."
2. *Encourage freewheeling.* The wilder the idea the better. It's easier to tame down a wild idea than it is to think up another one.
3. *Try for quantity.* The larger the number of ideas, the better the chance of getting good ones.
4. *Combine and improve.* Group members should state their own ideas. They should also suggest how the ideas of others could be turned into better ideas. Sometimes two or three ideas can be joined to form still another idea.

One person started a brainstorming session by saying:

- What new products not now available are needed for the home? Here is your opportunity to dream up all those gadgets, appliances, etc., that you believe would make home life more enjoyable.[2]

These are a few of the ideas generated in the session:[3]

- Suction cups on the bottom of egg beaters to prevent skidding in the bowl.
- Venetian blinds constructed so that the slats in the upper or lower half may be opened or closed independently of the other half.
- Switches for doorbells so you can turn them off when children are asleep or when you don't want to be disturbed.

Get together with two or three people to practice brainstorming. Start with the statement: Name as many uses as you can for empty plastic household detergent bottles. How many did you list in your group? It will be interesting to compare your list with those of other groups in the class.

---

1. Adapted from Alex F. Osborn, *Applied Imagination,* 3d ed. (New York: Charles Scribner's Sons, 1963), 156.
2. Ibid., 174.
3. Ibid.

Even though brainstorming is used most often in groups, you can also use it alone. Follow these rules for individual brainstorming:

1. *Don't judge your own ideas until you have finished the list.* Never erase or scratch out an idea.
2. *Do some freewheeling.* Don't be afraid to write down some farfetched ideas.
3. *Try for quantity.* Remember, by writing down many ideas, you increase your chances of getting good ideas.
4. *Combine and improve.* Write down all ideas that come to mind. Then add to the list by combining and improving ideas.

MAKING OBSERVATIONS

An idea for a new enterprise may come from observing your own needs and wants or by observing the needs or wants of the people around you. For example, many of your friends may have said that no store in the area sells tapes and compact discs.

How observant are you? Before you answer that question, see if you can answer these questions:

1. On which corner is the name of your street posted?
2. What is the location of the fire hydrant closest to your school?
3. If there is a stairway in your home or school, how many steps does it have?

Even if you answered the three questions correctly, you may still agree that people do not always observe their surroundings. Observation is an active process. If you are not actively trying to observe, you probably will not observe.

Sharpen your observation skills, and you will improve your chances of finding new enterprise ideas. You can do this by the following actions:

1. *Watch trends, particularly those in food, clothing, and leisure-time activities.* Entrepreneurs have responded to people's interest in physical fitness by providing exercise clothing, equipment, and instruction. Some restaurants provide the nutritional information for their menu items. Be alert. Trends in other parts of the country may be clues to future trends in your area. What foods or clothing styles are moving from one part of the country to another?
2. *Observe faults or shortcomings in existing products, services, or businesses.* Did the store where you bought a gift provide a box for the item, and was gift-wrapping service available? Observing that many stores did not offer these services, entrepreneurs developed a new kind of business—an enterprise that would wrap gifts and, if needed, pack the item for shipping to another city. Busy people are willing to pay for these services.
3. *Look for new associations among objects, processes, and ideas.* See if you can take an idea from one line of business and use it in another.

Pizza shops have provided home delivery for years. Fast-food restaurants serving hamburgers or chicken, on the other hand, have not generally offered this service. Combine the two ideas to create a new concept, that of a hamburger or chicken restaurant that delivers to the home. Or, how about combining two ideas to establish a store that sells not only the latest books but also the tapes and compact discs that your friends are looking for?

4. *Observe that some things that used to be done very well are not being done any more.* At one time, gasoline stations could handle practically any automobile repair problem. Should somebody establish full-service gasoline stations in areas where they no longer exist?
5. *Try out your idea on other people.* Ideas must be tested. When you get an idea for a new product or service, plan to develop and refine it. This could take weeks, months, or even years. Tell your idea to your friends. Observe how they react to the idea and listen to what they say. Are they enthusiastic? Do they encourage you to keep working on the idea? Most important, do they think your product or service is a gimmick, or do they believe it has value?

KEEPING A NOTEBOOK OF IDEAS

Ideas for new enterprises can come to you at any time. They often come at times when you least expect them, such as while you are eating lunch, riding in a car, or watching television. In the following examples you will see when the ideas appeared for some well-known products and services:[4]

- The idea to build an outboard motor came to Ole Evinrude when ice cream melted in a boat he was rowing to a picnic on an island in Wisconsin one warm August day.
- The idea to form Diners Club came to Ralph Schneider one night when he was entertaining friends at a New York restaurant and found he had lost his wallet.
- The idea for the automatic toaster came to Charles Strite when he got mad at the burnt toast in the lunchroom of the factory where he worked as a mechanic.

Be prepared to catch ideas while they are alive and fresh in your mind. At the moment an idea appears it may seem that it would be impossible to forget it. Yet in a very short time it becomes blurred or is forgotten. As soon as you get an idea, write it down. Keep track of your ideas in a notebook. If you get an idea when you do not have your notebook with you, write it down on a scrap of paper. Then add the idea to the list in your notebook as soon as you can.

---

4. Adapted from Karl H. Vesper, *New Venture Strategies* (Englewood Cliffs, NJ: Prentice-Hall, 1980), 135.

Plan to spend time at least once each month to review your notebook of ideas and to answer these questions:

1. What are the advantages or benefits of each enterprise idea?
2. What are the disadvantages or drawbacks of each idea?
3. Does the great idea you had a few weeks ago still seem great?
4. Do the ideas have anything in common? For example, are several ideas related to computer software?
5. Does the list of ideas suggest that your interests are changing? Perhaps the enterprise idea you had several weeks ago was to start a small retail store. However, now you may be setting your sights on a large-scale manufacturing business.
6. What is the best idea in the notebook? Why?

PPLICATION OF CREATIVITY TO BUSINESS OPERATIONS

Many of the methods used to generate new enterprise ideas (i.e., "new things to do") can be adapted to find ways of making a business operate more efficiently (i.e., "new ways of doing things"). By conducting surveys, brainstorming, making observations, or keeping a notebook of ideas, entrepreneurs can identify new and improved methods of operating more profitably.

The people who are probably the most knowledgeable about making a business run more efficiently are the employees. Since they may spend eight hours a day at a particular task, it would be surprising if they did not find ways of doing it better. But unless employees are asked, it may never occur to them to share their ideas and suggestions. Entrepreneurs can conduct informal surveys as they walk around the workplace talking to employees and listening closely to what they are saying. Formal surveys can be conducted from time to time. Valuable information can also be obtained by surveying customers, suppliers, or other firms or individuals who have contact with the company.

Brainstorming can be an aid in helping a business run more smoothly. To encourage an unrestrained flow of ideas, follow the rules for brainstorming discussed earlier in this chapter. The following are examples of the types of questions that a retailer could use in a group brainstorming session:

- What can we do to serve customers faster?
- How can we reduce shoplifting?
- What steps can we take to reduce our investment in inventory?
- What methods would allow us to operate the warehouse with fewer employees?

Become an observer and you may get just the ideas you need to improve your business. Pay attention to what is going on around you. Watch competitors to learn all you can about how they operate. It's safe to assume that those who have been successful for several years must be doing things right, so it will be worth your time to observe and learn from them. Try to figure what makes them successful. Do their employees take pride in their work and do they appear to work more efficiently? Are customers served quickly and with a smile? You can also learn by observing the business practices of noncompetitors. To illustrate, owners and managers of businesses of all types and sizes have tried to train their employees to be as friendly and efficient as those who work at Disneyland and Walt Disney World.

Ideas for improving the operation of your business may come to you at any time, even at times when you least expect them. Ideas are fleeting and may leave your mind as fast as they enter. It is, therefore, important to write them down while you can still remember the details. Some people carry a small pocket-sized notebook in which to record ideas that come to them throughout the day. Others keep a notebook on the desk or next to the chair where they like to sit to read. Be prepared to write down every idea regardless of whether it is possible to implement it immediately or not. Unworkable ideas can be discarded later, but if you do not write down every idea right away, you run the risk that some of your best thoughts and ideas will be lost forever.

ACTION STEPS FOR ASPIRING ENTREPRENEURS

Use these action steps to help you prepare for the possibility of being an entrepreneur at some point in your career:

1. Develop your skill as a listener. Listen to what people are saying about the products and services they buy or would buy if they were available.
2. Read a special-interest magazine dealing with a topic that does not interest you. You may find an idea that you can use.
3. Search for solutions to negative trends such as air pollution or the lack of space in the nation's landfills to accommodate an endless stream of garbage and waste. These and other problems will have to be solved to keep our economy running efficiently.
4. Look at what's popular (e.g., clothing styles, foods, television shows), try to find out what makes them popular, and then predict what future trends might be.

Illustration 3-4
Entrepreneurial skills are needed to help solve society's problems.

BUILDING YOUR ENTERPRISE VOCABULARY

Match the following terms with the statements that best define the terms. Write the letter of your choice in the space provided.

a. classified advertising
b. business opportunity advertisements
c. business services advertisements
d. special-interest magazines
e. trade publications
f. trade shows
g. craft and hobby shows
h. survey
i. formal survey
j. brainstorming

_______ 1. Product exhibits open only to people engaged in a particular line of business or trade.
_______ 2. Advertising messages grouped together in one part of the newspaper.
_______ 3. Magazines and newspapers designed for people working within a particular business or field.
_______ 4. Messages used to reach potential customers by persons with specialized business or technical skills to sell.
_______ 5. A technique used to solve a problem by generating as many ideas as possible.
_______ 6. Descriptions of the enterprise to be sold, the location, and sometimes the selling price.
_______ 7. Places where people show others what they do in their spare time.
_______ 8. Publications that contain articles and advertisements in specific areas of interest.
_______ 9. A means of obtaining information by either interviewing a number of people or asking them to complete a questionnaire.
_______ 10. A means of obtaining information by asking a number of people a series of questions and then summarizing their answers.

UNDERSTANDING KEY CONCEPTS

Write a short answer to each of the questions below.

1. How can business opportunity advertisements help you if your career plans are uncertain?

____

____

____

2. What types of newspaper articles should you read when looking for new enterprise ideas?

____

____

____

3. Why are trade publications good sources of new enterprise ideas?

4. Describe the differences between public shows and trade shows. Give an example of each type of show.

5. List two ways you can make an informal survey.

6. What is the meaning of this statement: "The existence of several businesses of one type does not necessarily mean you should not start a similar enterprise"?

7. List the four rules for individual brainstorming.

8. What are five ways to sharpen your observation skills?

9. Explain how creativity can be used to improve business operations.

APPLYING YOUR ENTERPRISE KNOWLEDGE

These activities will give you a chance to apply what you have learned in Chapter 3.

1. In this activity you will use "business opportunities" and "business services" advertisements from a newspaper of your choice. You may want to use a Sunday edition as it usually contains more advertisements than a daily edition.

   a. Read the "business opportunities" advertisements in one issue of a newspaper and identify five different businesses that interest you. In the space below, list the five businesses and tell why you selected each.

Type of Business	Why You Are Interested in It
1. ______	
2. ______	
3. ______	
4 ______	
5. ______	

   b. Read "business services" advertisements in one issue of a newspaper and identify five different businesses that interest you. In the space below, list the five businesses and tell why you selected each.

Type of Business	Why You Are Interested in It
1. ______	
2. ______	
3. ______	
4 ______	
5. ______	

2. List at least five questions you would ask consumers to find out if they are satisfied with auto repair businesses.

   ______

   ______

   ______

   ______

3. The purpose of this activity is to give you practice in brainstorming. As soon as you have completed part a, you may start part b.

   a. During the next five minutes, list as many ideas for new enterprises as you can.

   b. Review your list of ideas for new enterprises and cross out those that you would not want to own and operate.

4. As a consumer, you've probably had a chance to observe how grocery stores operate. You're familiar with their products and services. Suggest three specific ways grocery store owners and managers could improve their stores.

5. Compact disc and book clubs offer their members a different selection each month. Could this idea be applied to other businesses? List three other products that could be sold this way.

SOLVING BUSINESS PROBLEMS: FOUR CORNERS PARTNERS

Ann, Brenda, Charlie, and Diane have been friends for almost two years. They met when they were all assigned to the same unit at the military base near Springfield. Within the next six months, they will all be completing their enlistments, and they will be leaving military service. Charlie and Ann each have sixty days left to serve. Diane has four months left and Brenda has almost six months.

The four friends agree that their military service has been a valuable experience. At the same time, each of them is looking forward to pursuing a career as a civilian. They often talk of starting their own businesses. Recently, they have been talking about going into business together. This is a possibility because they all want to stay in Springfield.

At lunch on Monday, Charlie said, "Let's meet for at least two hours each week to talk about a business we could open together. At least for now, why don't we call ourselves the Four Corners Partners. It's a good name because each one of us grew up in a different part, or corner, of the United States."

With only sixty days to prepare for his return to civilian life, Charlie is eager to plan his career. He continued, "If we're serious about going into business together, and I think we are, we should get some plans on paper real soon." Ann said, "I agree, but we can't start planning until we decide what business we want to start. I think we should do some brainstorming when we meet next week. That should give us many business ideas to consider." "Great suggestion," Charlie commented, "but I think we should agree on some rules for the brainstorming meeting; otherwise it'll get out of hand. I was in one of those meetings once. The whole discussion went off in several directions." Brenda came into the discussion and said to Charlie, "Go ahead and suggest some rules." "All right," Charlie said, "here are two rules: First, we should each come prepared with a list of ideas so we won't waste time trying to think up ideas at the meeting. Second, no wild ideas will be allowed. If we follow these rules, I think we'll have a good brainstorming session."

1. Do you agree with Charlie that each person should come to the brainstorming meeting with a list of ideas? Why or why not?

2. What will happen if wild ideas are not allowed? Explain.

3. Describe how you would set up and conduct the brainstorming meeting.

BUSINESS PLAN PROJECT

Answer the following questions in the space provided on pages 81 and 82.

1. What name have you chosen for your new enterprise?
2. In what major field of business activity is the enterprise?
3. Where will the enterprise be located? If you do not know the exact location, describe the type of location needed.
4. What products or services will you provide?
5. Who are your main competitors?
6. What benefits will you offer customers that competing enterprises do not offer?
7. What background and experience do you have to start the enterprise? If you do not have the appropriate skills now, how will you acquire them?
8. Will you employ other people at the beginning of the business? If so, how many and what tasks will they perform?

BUSINESS PLAN
prepared by

____

Name of Enterprise: ______________________________

Field of Business Activity: ______________________________

Location: ______________________________

____

____

Products or Services: ______________________________

____

____

____

____

Competition: ______________________________

____

____

____

____

____

Customer Benefits: ______________________________

____

____

____

____

____

Management Expertise:

Personnel:

CHAPTER 4

ANALYZING MARKETS AND COMPETITORS

Customers do not buy things, they buy solutions to problems. One person may buy a bicycle to solve a transportation problem. Another person may buy a bicycle to solve an exercise, or lack-of-exercise, problem. The purpose of a business, therefore, is to help people solve problems.

Your enterprise will be just one of many businesses competing for customers. To survive and prosper, you will have to look constantly for better ways to help people solve their problems. Maybe you will provide a new service, make a new product, or design a new and more convenient package for an old product. Whatever you do, you will need customers, perhaps many of them. Without customers who want your product or service and are willing and able to pay your price, there is no need to be in business.

To help customers solve their problems, you will have to learn about the customers and the markets of which they are a part. Because other businesses will probably be trying to do the same thing, you will also have to find out as much as you can about the other businesses. In this chapter, you will learn methods of analyzing your markets and your competitors.

Learning Objectives

After you have studied Chapter 4, you should be able to:

1. Describe the process of market segmentation.
2. Explain sales forecasting.
3. Identify the characteristics of a good location.
4. Evaluate the competition.

ENTREPRENEUR PROFILE Debbi Fields

Debbi Fields, the founder of Mrs. Fields, Inc., is probably the world's best-known maker of chocolate chip cookies. She is an entrepreneur who describes her personal philosophy of achievement with two phrases: "Good enough never is," and "If you chase money you'll never catch it." Inspired by this philosophy, 20-year-old Debbi opened her first cookie store in 1977 in Palo Alto, California.

Born Debra Sivyer, Debbi and her four sisters grew up in a working-class neighborhood in Oakland, California. Her father was a welder at a U.S. naval base and her mother was a homemaker who could "make a dollar stretch forever."

As a teenager Debbi made one of the most important discoveries of her life. She discovered the value of work and the satisfaction of doing a good job. Through part-time jobs she gained the confidence that she could compete in the workplace.

When she was 13 years old Debbi was hired as foul-line ball girl for the Oakland A's. Her job was to retrieve foul balls hit to the third-base side of the field, a job she performed in front of thousands of people.

In her job with the Oakland A's Debbi learned that being in the public eye is not threatening and can actually be enjoyable. She also learned that everyone on earth needs to feel important. This lesson was the result of watching how different baseball players responded to requests for autographs from kids. Some players willingly signed, while others did not want to be bothered and were cold and rude to the kids. This behavior made Debbi furious because she saw it made the kids feel unimportant. Translating it into business terms, Debbi did not believe that these players were giving their customers (i.e., the fans) the service they deserved.

Debbi's next job was at Mervyn's department store, where she worked after school and on weekends as a part-time sales clerk in the boys' department. Here she gained first-hand experience in finding out what customers wanted and then in providing it to them.

From childhood through her teenage years, Debbi spent many hours baking chocolate chip cookies that were quickly devoured by her family and friends. At first she followed the recipe printed on the bag of chocolate chips; then later, she created her own recipe by experimenting with the ingredients. Debbi made a major change in the recipe when she was 17 years old: she started using butter instead of margarine. This change was, in her words, "fantastic."

Debbi married Randy Fields who, coincidentally, loved chocolate chip cookies. So Debbi kept baking and continued making changes in the recipe. Her next innovation was to make larger cookies. By the time she was 18, Debbi had perfected the chocolate chip cookie.

With Randy busy with his corporate career, Debbi looked for a constructive use of her time and energy. She did not have to look far. Because she was so good at baking cookies, Debbi decided to open a cookie shop. However, Debbi received little or no support for the idea. She discussed the business idea with her parents, her mother-in-law, her friends, and even various business professionals. While they all thought her cookies were delicious, they did not believe she could make a successful business out of selling cookies through her own store. Although he did not say it in so many words, Debbi knew that Randy did not believe the idea would work. Nevertheless, he went to the bank with her to get a $50,000 loan to start the business. Debbi was then 20 years old.

The name for the business was the product of an evolutionary process. The first name Debbi came up with was "The Chocolate Chippery," followed by "Debbi's Chocolate Chippery." Then Randy suggested "Mrs. Fields Chocolate Chippery," a name that Debbi liked because it had a friendly sound to it. The first store was opened on

August 18, 1977, in Palo Alto, California. Sometime later the name was simplified to "Mrs. Fields Cookies."

The second store was opened in 1979 and a third in 1980. By this time there was little doubt that the company would grow rapidly. Mrs. Fields Cookies would soon be a household word. By 1986, Randy had quit his job so he could work with Debbi in the cookie business. In 1987 alone, 173 stores were opened, bringing the total number in the company to 543, including stores in Japan and Australia. Also in 1987, the company had earnings of $18 million on sales of $104 million.

The success of Mrs. Fields Cookies did not continue into 1988. That year the company suffered a net loss of $19 million. The company was suffering the pains of the previous few years' rapid expansion. Stores were too close together in some areas and some stores were not placed in the right location. As a result, nearly 100 stores had to be closed in 1988.

Debbi realized that mistakes had been made, she determined what those mistakes were, and, most important, she learned from them. She decided to spend considerably less time on the day-to-day details and much more time guiding the direction of the company, including looking for new business opportunities. One of the newest lines of business the company has entered is known as Mrs. Fields Bakeries, featuring muffins, bread, sandwiches, and soups. Debbi still believes in experimenting with recipes. The company is currently testing Desserve, a reduced-calorie ingredient developed by the NutraSweet subsidiary of the Monsanto Company. By the early 1990s the company had reached an annual sales volume of over $100 million with a work force of 5,000 people.

Source: Debbi Fields and Alan Furst, "One Smart Cookie": How a housewife's chocolate chip recipe turned into a multimillion-dollar business—the story of Mrs. Fields Cookies *(New York: Simon & Schuster, 1987); Katherine Weisman, "Succeeding by Failing,"* Forbes *(June 25, 1990): 160; and* Ward's Business Directory of U.S. Private and Public Companies *(Detroit: Gale Research, Inc., 1992).*

ANALYZING MARKETS

The word ***market*** is sometimes confusing because it seems to have so many meanings. In newspaper headlines you may have read, "Investors put more money into the stock market," "Job market tight in many cities," or "Commercial real estate market improves." Television newscasters often mention the new car market or the international market. We buy groceries in a supermarket. These are just a few of the markets you hear about every day.

THE MARKET FOR AN ENTERPRISE

Before you decide to start a new enterprise, you will have to identify your market. In this sense, ***market*** refers to the groups of people, businesses, or organizations seeking the types of products or services you sell. Customers must also be both willing and able to pay the price you charge; otherwise, they would not be a part of your market.

Persons or households that buy products and services for personal or family use are called ***consumers.*** They buy products from a wide variety of sources, including retail stores, mail-order companies, and door-to-door salespeople. Customers also buy services from such enterprises as auto repair shops, restaurants, cable television companies, photography studios, and car rental firms.

Business users are companies or institutions that buy products and services to use in running their businesses, to resell, to produce other products, or to provide services. Schools buy desks, floor wax, and paper. Sporting goods stores buy baseball bats, athletic shoes, and tennis rackets to resell to customers. Wholesale grocers buy from food producers and resell to supermarkets. Furniture manufacturers buy wood and upholstery fabric to make tables, chairs, and sofas. Car rental firms buy cars to provide service to their customers. These are examples of the many purchases business users make each day.

MARKET SEGMENTS

Some entrepreneurs start out trying to meet the needs of every possible customer. In other words, they try to be "all things to all people." They scatter their efforts and energy. In the end, they do not serve anyone very well. A better way is to concentrate your efforts on market segments. ***Market segments*** are groups of people with similar needs and characteristics. Think of the market as a pie and a market segment as one piece.

You will need information to help you as you undertake the task of identifying market segments, forecasting sales, finding a location, and evaluating the competition. The Small Business Administration and other sources of this type of information are discussed in the "Sources of Assistance" section of Chapter 5.

Dividing the market for a product or a service into segments is ***market segmentation.*** Each segment consists of customers who are alike in many ways. The particular group to whom you wish to sell your products or services is your ***target market.***

Large corporations offering different products often have several target markets. Each of the domestic automobile manufacturers, for example, produces several models. Each model is usually designed to meet the needs and preferences of people in a particular target market. However, when starting a new business, the best advice is to select just one target market. When, and if, you are successful in serving that one group, you can start thinking about other target markets.

Learn as much as possible about your target market. You can do this by asking yourself these questions:

1. Will my customers be consumers or business users?
2. If they are consumers, how old are they? How much money do they earn? Where do they live? Are they in cities, suburbs, or rural areas? Are they more likely to be men or women?
3. If they are business users, are they extractive, manufacturing, wholesaling, retailing, or service enterprises?

4. What needs will the product or service satisfy for customers?
5. How many potential customers are in the area where I will open my business?
6. Where do these potential customers now buy the products or services I want them to buy from me?
7. What price are the customers willing to pay?
8. What can I do for customers that competitors are not doing for them?

Illustration 4-1
Target markets come in all types and sizes.

© Lawrence Manning/Westlight

Develop a mental picture of customers in your target market. Then try to put yourself in their place and see your enterprise as they see it. Do this when you start your business and do it every day you are in business. Never stop studying your market, because it will continually change. Neighborhoods change, customers' needs and buying habits change, and new products replace old products.

SALES FORECASTS

Forecasting sales is essential for every business enterprise, regardless of its size or the field of activity. The forecast is the basis of sound planning. Without it, you will not know how much merchandise or raw material to buy, how many employees to hire, or how much money you will need.

WHAT IS A SALES FORECAST? A ***sales forecast*** is an estimate of sales, in dollars or units, for a specific time period. The forecast may be for a specific item or service, or for the enterprise's total sales volume. One year is the most widely used time period. However, some entrepreneurs prepare sales forecasts for periods of three or six months.

Forecasts of less than a year are often desirable when sales fluctuate widely from month to month. Sellers of seasonal products or services often find that it is not practical to look ahead a full year. Some product examples are fashion clothing, lawn and garden supplies, and home appliances such as room air conditioners and freezers.

Review sales forecasts frequently and revise them as necessary. New competitors, or price changes by existing competitors, can make your estimates obsolete. Therefore, many businesspersons review their annual sales forecasts monthly. In this way, they can respond quickly to changes that affect the enterprise.

HOW IS A SALES FORECAST PREPARED? The first step in forecasting sales is to estimate the market potential for your products and services. The term ***market potential*** refers to the total sales of all similar businesses in your area. In other words, market potential is the total of your sales and those of your competitors.

To determine market potential, be prepared to go to several sources for information. Start by visiting the local chamber of commerce and the library. Also, contact the trade association for your line of business. Virtually every industry has such an association; ask those who are already in business for the address. The information from these sources is usually in the form of nationwide averages. That is, the information may not refer specifically to your local area. Nevertheless, the information is useful because it can give you the background for further study of your market.

Next, you should seek the help of a banker and an accountant. These individuals are familiar with the sales and finances of a wide range of enterprises. For this reason, they can help you to estimate the potential for your market.

Other potential sources of information are those businesses that sell to enterprises similar to yours. Examples are manufacturers, wholesalers, and suppliers who conduct business regularly in the community.

Finally, locate an entrepreneur in your line of business but not in your community. Because you will not be competitors, this person may be willing to share information about market potential.

After you have estimated the market potential, you should estimate your share of the market. This will be your sales forecast. The estimate is important because it is the basis for almost all other decisions you will make.

Suppose, for example, that you are starting a printing business. You want to specialize in business cards, letterheads, envelopes, business forms, and menus. You find that $600,000 is spent on this kind of printing each year in your community. This is the market potential.

There are five printing shops; but when you open yours, there will be six competing businesses. To compute ***average market share,*** divide market potential by the number of competing businesses. Using numbers from the example, the computation would be as follows:

$$\text{Average Market Share} = \frac{\text{Market Potential}}{\text{Number of Competing Businesses}}$$

$$= \frac{\$600{,}000}{6} = \$100{,}000$$

The average market share is $100,000. You should not assume that you will reach this level of sales your first year. You are new and the other businesses are established. However, you should try to estimate how much of that $100,000 you can get. You can do this by observing competitors to find answers to these questions:

1. What are their successful sales points?
2. What are their weaknesses?
3. What can you provide that they do not provide?
4. How much business can you actually take away from competitors? (Avoid the tendency to overestimate this figure.)

Based on these answers, you may estimate that your sales will be $70,000 for the first year. The estimate is not as high as average market share, but you are just getting established.

Review your initial estimate no later than three months after opening. At that time, you may have to adjust the estimate either upward or downward.

For example, because of superior products and services, you may be taking more business away from competitors than originally planned; or the total market potential may have increased because there are new customers in the area. These factors would call for an increase in your sales forecast.

On the other hand, you may have to decrease the forecast. For example, a new competitor may be in town; or maybe not all your equipment was installed on time.

LOCATION

Location is the place where you have your main base of operation. Wherever you locate, make sure the community needs the business you want to start. Deciding on the location for a new enterprise involves three steps. You must (1) choose a community or city, (2) choose an area within the community or city, and (3) choose a specific site in the area.

CHOOSE A COMMUNITY OR CITY. Certain communities are more desirable than others as locations for new enterprises. In choosing a community, you should consider (1) personal factors, (2) population, (3) level of employment, (4) competition, and (5) legal considerations.

Personal Factors. One of the advantages of being an entrepreneur is that you can choose where you will work. You are free to pick a place where it would be pleasant to live. Factors that make a community pleasant often make it a good place for conducting business. Look at the general appearance of the town. Are most homes neat, and are streets and parks well maintained? What about public transportation and public utilities (such as water, electricity, and sewage)? Do these services meet local needs? Determine the quality of schools as well as police and fire protection. In short, find out if residents take pride in their community.

Illustration 4-2
Attractive surroundings can help a business succeed.

Population. A community's population is an important factor in choosing a location. Are there enough customers for your products or services? Is the population growing or declining? Given the choice, you will probably want to locate in a fast-growing city. Construction of new homes, apartments, and shopping facilities is an indication of growth.

Level of Employment. Spending for some goods and services is low in cities where many persons are unemployed. Cities with unemployment problems tend to be poor locations for businesses intending to sell to local consumers, such as appliance stores and auto dealerships. The same cities, however, could be good locations for other businesses. One example is the entrepreneur who will hire many employees for a manufacturing company. Local conditions would not affect a product sold in other cities. Another example is the base of operation for a mail-order firm selling goods all over the country.

Competition. Overcrowding occurs in many fields of business activity. Therefore, you should be concerned with the nature and amount of local competition. Determine the number, size, and quality of competitors. Then decide if there is likely to be room for your new enterprise.

Legal Considerations. Some cities and states try to attract new businesses by offering tax advantages. Others have unusually high taxes or restrict certain businesses. Taxes and restrictions mean higher costs of operating a business. You should, therefore, inquire about these items when considering a location. Also, check on zoning ordinances that limit your selection of sites in the town.

CHOOSE AN AREA WITHIN THE COMMUNITY OR CITY. After choosing a city in which to locate, the next step is to choose an area within the city. Your goal will be to find an area that is suited to your type of enterprise.

The location decision is more important for some types of business than for others. For example, a shoe store should be conveniently located for shoppers. If it is hard to find, customers will not make the effort to shop there. On the other hand, a carpet cleaning service's location is of minor importance. Why? Because the service is performed in the home, and customers do not have to go to the place of business.

Your location decision will depend on whether your enterprise is manufacturing, wholesaling, retailing, or services. Extractive enterprises are usually locked into a fixed location where products are found in nature.

Manufacturing. Manufacturers usually need access to low-cost forms of transportation. For example, railroad sidings or trucking companies should be nearby. This makes it convenient for receiving raw materials and shipping finished products. Access to utilities, such as electricity, water, and sewers, is also important.

Wholesaling. Like manufacturers, wholesalers should have access to various transportation facilities. They should also be located in the middle of the market they serve. The wholesalers will then be conveniently located for quick shipments to all customers.

Retailing. Retail store locations are largely determined by the type of merchandise carried. For example, men's and women's clothing stores are commonly located near department stores. As another example, home furnishings stores and furniture stores are located near each other. Preferred locations for other retailers are on the main traffic thoroughfares. Examples are supermarkets and drugstores.

If you go into retailing, locate in an area where customers are most likely to shop for the kind of goods you sell.

Services. Personal services and repair services have many of the location requirements of retail stores. Dry cleaners, travel agencies, and auto repair shops must be located where customers can come conveniently. Likewise, business services, such as equipment rental firms and accounting firms, usually locate in the business districts nearest their customers.

CHOOSE A SPECIFIC SITE. The choice of a specific site is less critical for manufacturing and wholesaling concerns than it is for retail and service businesses. Therefore, the following discussion on site choice applies primarily to the latter two fields of business activity.

You may find very few specific sites that are vacant. This could mean that you will have to take whatever site is available. Before you make a final decision, you should answer these questions:

1. Is parking space adequate for the enterprise?
2. Is the building, as well as those nearby, attractive and well maintained?
3. Can cars enter and leave the parking lot with ease?
4. Is there an ample flow of traffic on nearby streets?
5. Is the rent or building cost high or low in relation to the area?
6. Are there any restrictions on the use of the property?

You should use a "score sheet" when evaluating different sites. Some of the factors listed in the score sheet in Figure 4-1 are more important for certain enterprises than for others. Start with this score sheet, then eliminate factors or add new factors to meet your needs.

Figure 4-1
Score Sheet on Sites

Score Sheet on Sites

Grade each factor: "A" for excellent, "B" for good, "C" for fair, "D" for poor.

Factor	Grade
1. Centrally located to reach my market	______
2. Merchandise or raw materials available readily	______
3. Nearby competition situation	______
4. Transportation availability and rates	______
5. Quantity of available employees	______
6. Prevailing rates of employee pay	______
7. Parking facilities	______
8. Adequacy of utilities (sewer, water, power)	______
9. Traffic flow	______
10. Taxation burden	______
11. Quality of police and fire protection	______
12. Housing availability for employees	______
13. Environmental factors (schools, cultural and community activities, kinds of businesses nearby)	______
14. Physical suitability of building	______
15. Type and cost of lease	______
16. Provision for future expansion	______
17. Overall estimate of quality of site in 10 years	______

Source: Wendell O. Metcalf for the U.S. Small Business Administration, Starting and Managing a Small Business of Your Own, *3d ed., The Starting and Managing Series, vol. 1 (Washington, DC: U.S. Government Printing Office, 1973), 27.*

STUDYING THE COMPETITION

Practically all business enterprises in the United States face competition. ***Competition*** is the effort of two or more businesses to win the same group of people as customers. Individual firms involved are called ***competitors.*** A new enterprise will survive only if it offers some competitive advantages. Examples are better service, superior product, lower price, or shorter delivery time. Customers buy from a particular enterprise for these and other advantages. It is important, therefore, to include a study of competition in your business plan. This study should include the number of competitors as well as their strengths and weaknesses.

NUMBER OF SIMILAR BUSINESSES

Who are your competitors? How many are there? You should be aware that not all competitors are located in your community. For example, if you open a gift shop, you may be competing with companies selling gifts by mail order; or you may have local competitors whose enterprises are not exactly like yours. As an example, the gift department in a department store could be a major competitor. When planning your enterprise, you must identify the competition.

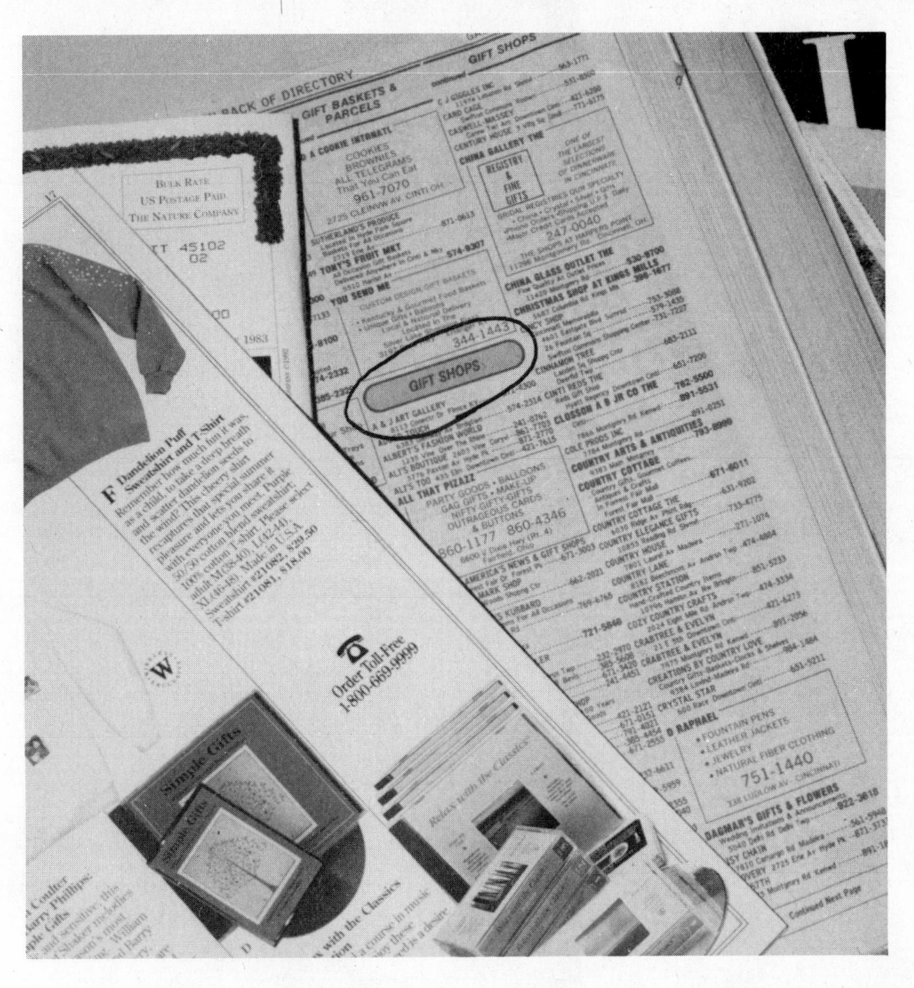

Illustration 4-3
When planning an enterprise, identify the competition.

You should also determine if the local area already has too many enterprises like the one you plan to open. A relationship exists between the number of people in a community and the number of businesses of various kinds. Figure 4-2 shows how the number of community inhabitants per store varies by the kind of business. For instance, there is one hardware store for every 12,499 inhabitants and one shoe store for every 6,410 inhabitants. On the other hand, there is only one camera and photographic supply store for every 62,494 inhabitants. These averages are based on nationwide census data and may not necessarily be true for your local area. However, they can be used as guidelines when deciding if your community has too many businesses of a certain type.

Figure 4-2
Number of Inhabitants per Store by Selected Kinds of Business (national averages)

Kind of Business	Number of Inhabitants per Store
BUILDING MATERIALS, HARDWARE, AND GARDEN SUPPLIES	
Building materials, supply stores	6,578
Hardware stores	12,499
Retail nurseries, lawn and garden supply stores	22,725
Mobile home dealers	49,995
GENERAL MERCHANDISE STORES	
Department stores	24,998
Variety stores	24,998
Miscellaneous general merchandise stores	16,665
FOOD STORES	
Grocery stores	1,811
Meat and fish (seafood) stores	22,725
Retail bakeries	11,363
Fruit stores, vegetable markets	83,325
Candy, nut, confectionery stores	41,663
AUTOMOTIVE DEALERS	
Motor vehicle dealers–new and used cars	8,928
Motor vehicle dealers–used cars only	16,665
Auto and home supply stores	5,434
Boat dealers	49,995
Recreational and utility trailer dealers	83,325
Motorcycle dealers	62,494
Gasoline service stations	2,174
APPAREL AND ACCESSORY STORES	
Men's and boys' clothing, furnishings	14,704
Women's clothing and specialty stores and furriers	4,166
Women's ready-to-wear stores	4,807
Family clothing stores	13,888
Shoe stores	6,410
Children's and infants' wear stores	41,663
FURNITURE, HOME FURNISHINGS, AND EQUIPMENT STORES	
Furniture stores	7,575
Home furnishings stores	7,812
Household appliance stores	22,725
Radio, television, computer, and music stores	7,352
EATING AND DRINKING PLACES	
Restaurants and lunchrooms	1,613
Refreshment places	1,811

Figure 4-2 (*continued*)

MISCELLANEOUS RETAIL STORES	
Drug and proprietary stores	4,807
Used merchandise stores	16,665
Sporting goods, bicycle shops	11,363
Book stores	22,725
Stationery stores	49,995
Jewelry stores	8,928
Hobby, toy, game shops	24,998
Camera, photographic supply	62,494
Gift, novelty, and souvenir shops	7,812
Sewing, needlework, piece goods	24,998
Mail-order houses	35,711
Automatic merchandising machine operators	49,995
Direct selling establishments	22,725
Fuel dealers	19,229
Florists	9,258
Optical goods stores	17,855

Source: U.S. Bureau of the Census, Statistical Abstract of the United States: 1991, *111th ed. (Washington, DC: U.S. Government Printing Office, 1991), 7, 768.*

STRENGTHS AND WEAKNESSES OF COMPETITORS

Once you have identified your competitors, you should determine the strengths and weaknesses of each. Visit each competitor's place of business. Observe the competitor's operation and the way customers are treated.

After each visit, make notes of your observations. Then summarize the information when you have completed the series of visits. The table in Figure 4-3 may be helpful in comparing various competitors. For example, if the circled ratings described your three competitors, you would conclude that Competitor B would be your strongest competition.

Even though a comparison of competitors can be helpful, the information can become outdated. Competitors may make changes in their businesses. One may lower its prices while another increases the number of services it offers to customers. New competitors may open their doors, while others close theirs forever.

What will other businesses do when you start your business and begin competing against them? You should expect other businesses to react. Be prepared to take action. Plan ahead by writing scenarios. A ***scenario*** is an outline of a chain of events that an individual believes could possibly occur in the future. Collect all the information you can to prepare informed opinions. Ask experts for their opinions. Then write scenarios about your competition.

Because it is an attempt to describe the future, a single scenario will not be 100 percent accurate, nor is it expected to be. Write at least two scenarios: one for the worst case and one for the probable

Figure 4-3
Comparison of Competitors

Elements to Be Compared	Competitor A	Competitor B	Competitor C
Market share percentage	20 %	55 %	25 %
Product or service quality	Good / (Fair) / Poor	(Good) / Fair / Poor	Good / (Fair) / Poor
Location	Good / Fair / (Poor)	(Good) / Fair / Poor	Good / Fair / (Poor)
Size of facility	Large / Medium / (Small)	Large / (Medium) / Small	Large / Medium / (Small)
Prices	(High) / Average / Low	High / (Average) / Low	(High) / Average / Low
Reputation	Good / (Fair) / Poor	(Good) / Fair / Poor	Good / (Fair) / Poor
Number of years in business	8 years	22 years	6 years

case. In a ***worst-case scenario,*** try to imagine a situation as bad as it could get. Assume that your pizza restaurant is on one corner of an intersection. A worst-case scenario might be as follows: Competing pizza restaurants open up on each of the other three corners. Their quality is equal to yours; their prices are lower than yours. The new businesses advertise more than you do. The events described in the scenario may not occur. Nevertheless, you should think about what you would do if you actually had competitors across the street.

A ***probable-case scenario*** describes what is more likely to occur. Let's continue with the pizza shop example to determine a probable-case scenario: Competing businesses open up in the area, but the closest one is at least a mile from your location. A shop that starts out with lower prices gradually increases prices and now charges what you charge. You lose some customers to competitors, but you gain other customers by promoting your product and providing good customer service.

Illustration 4-4
Having competitors nearby can be a problem—or an opportunity.

ACTION STEPS FOR ASPIRING ENTREPRENEURS

Follow these action steps to help you prepare for a career as an entrepreneur:

1. Name one or two problems you believe a business could solve by providing a specific product or service.
2. Describe a lesson you learned from reading about Debbi Fields' experiences as an entrepreneur.
3. Select the community or city where you would like to start your business.
4. Make it a point to watch how businesses react when their competitors open in new locations or introduce new products or services.

BUILDING YOUR ENTERPRISE VOCABULARY

Match the following terms with the statements that best describe applications of those terms. Write the letter of your choice in the space provided.

a. business users
b. worst-case scenario
c. competition
d. market segments
e. probable-case scenario
f. target market
g. sales forecast
h. market potential
i. average market share
j. competitors

_______ 1. New technology could make the product that you sell obsolete.
_______ 2. Each year, $7 million worth of tires are sold in this area.
_______ 3. You and each of your nine competitors could expect to sell $200,000 worth of software this year and would, therefore, account for all $2 million of sales in the area.
_______ 4. A pizza shop increases spending on advertising in an attempt to lure customers away from the pizza shop across the street.
_______ 5. A seller of swimming pool chemicals anticipates sales of $950,000 for June, July, and August.
_______ 6. "New competitors may open up in the next few years; however, they are not likely to hurt our sales because we will be well established by then."
_______ 7. Families with children under two years of age.
_______ 8. The twelve quick oil-change and lube shops in town.
_______ 9. "We're concentrating our sales efforts on those customers whom we truly understand and know how to serve."
_______ 10. A wholesaler buys computer paper to resell to office supplies stores.

UNDERSTANDING KEY CONCEPTS

Write a short answer to each of the following questions.

1. What is the difference between consumers and business users?

____

____

____

____

____

2. One of your friends asks, "Shouldn't a business try to be all things to all people?" What is your answer?

____

____

3. List eight questions you can ask to learn as much as possible about your target market.

4. Why is a sales forecast important to a new enterprise?

5. Describe the steps in the sales forecasting process.

6. List the five factors you should consider when selecting the community or city in which to locate a new enterprise.

7. What two items should be included in a study of competition?

8. What is a scenario? How can a scenario be used to analyze competitors?

APPLYING YOUR ENTERPRISE KNOWLEDGE

These activities will give you a chance to apply what you have learned in Chapter 4.

1. Name three different businesses in your community. Then briefly describe the market segment served by each.

BUSINESS #1

Name of business: ______________________________

Description of market segment served: ______________________________

____

BUSINESS #2

Name of business: ______________________________

Description of market segment served: ______________________________

____

BUSINESS #3

Name of business: ______________________________

Description of market segment served: ______________________________

____

2. Suppose you are interested in starting an enterprise to sell auto and truck tires. You find that $1,500,000 is spent on tires each year in your community. Five enterprises are in the tire business at the present time. What would the average market share be if you decide to start your business?

____

____

____

____

3. Identify three to five potential customers for your enterprise. Ask them to describe the location where they prefer to buy the products or services you will sell. Then summarize their answers in the space provided.

CUSTOMER INTERVIEWS

Customer #1: ____________________

____

____

____

____

Customer #2: ____________________

____

____

____

____

Customer #3: ____________________

____

____

____

____

Customer #4: ____________________

____

____

____

____

Customer #5: ____________________

____

____

____

____

SOLVING BUSINESS PROBLEMS: AKEMI'S CREATIONS, INC.

Akemi became interested in the mail-order business after she read a magazine article about the increasing number of people who prefer to shop from the comfort of their homes. She also learned that these customers usually have little time available for shopping. Because they are often in the growing number of two-income families, these people often have more cash to spend than other customers. According to experts quoted in the article, start-up costs are relatively low for many mail-order enterprises, while profits are nearly double those earned by other forms of retailing.

Akemi had been designing and making stuffed animals, first as a hobby and later as a way to make extra money. When she started selling everything she could make, her sideline job turned into a full-time job and she started her business. Akemi's Creations, Inc., now has several employees to produce the stuffed animals. Akemi does all the designing, manages business operations, and travels to trade shows where she displays her stuffed animals and accepts orders from retailers. Her products are sold in toy and department stores in several states.

Akemi's Creations, Inc., has been making money even though most of the company's growth has been unplanned. What started out as a hobby became a profit-making business venture in a short time. Akemi wants to make sure that her business continues to grow. In addition, she believes that the mail-order business should be a major part of that planning. She realizes she will face new, and probably more aggressive, competition.

Assume that Akemi has asked you to help her analyze what her competition will be in the mail-order business. She wants to develop a comparison of competitors. Your task is to identify the elements to be compared.

BUSINESS PLAN PROJECT

Use the space on pages 105-108 for the following business plan activities.

1. Describe your target market by answering as many of these questions as you can:
   a. Will your customers be consumers or business users?
   b. If they are consumers, how old are they? How much money do they earn? Where do they live? Are they in cities, suburbs, or rural areas? Are they more likely to be men or women?
   c. If they are business users, are they extractive, manufacturing, wholesaling, retailing, or service enterprises?
   d. What needs will the product or service satisfy for customers?
   e. How many potential customers are in the area where you will open your business?
   f. Where do these potential customers now buy the products or services you want them to buy from you?
   g. What price are the customers willing to pay?

2. Describe the sales potential for your business by answering these questions:
   a. What is the average market share with your business included?
   b. What is your sales forecast for the first year in business?

3. Describe your location:
   a. Where do you plan to locate your business?
   b. Give the reasons for choosing that location.

4. Compare three of your potential competitors. You may wish to include one or two additional elements for comparison.

5. Write a worst-case scenario and a probable-case scenario about your competition.

DESCRIPTION OF TARGET MARKET

____

____

____

____

____

SALES POTENTIAL

Average market share: $ ________

First-year sales forecast: $ ________

LOCATION

The location of my enterprise is: ______________________________

I chose this location because: ______________________________

____

____

COMPARISON OF COMPETITORS

	Competitor A	Competitor B	Competitor C
Market share percentage	____%	____%	____%
Product or service quality	Good Fair Poor	Good Fair Poor	Good Fair Poor
Location	Good Fair Poor	Good Fair Poor	Good Fair Poor
Size of facility	Large Medium Small	Large Medium Small	Large Medium Small
Prices	High Average Low	High Average Low	High Average Low
Reputation	Good Fair Poor	Good Fair Poor	Good Fair Poor
Number of years in business	____ years	____ years	____ years
*			
*			

*Use these spaces for additional elements.

SCENARIOS OF COMPETITION

Worst case: ______________________________

Probable case: ____

CHAPTER 5

PLANNING A NEW ENTERPRISE

Knowing what you want to accomplish is the first step in planning a new enterprise. Once you have a clear idea of the enterprise, you can develop guidelines for action.

Learning Objectives

After you have studied Chapter 5, you should be able to:

1. Write a definition of your planned business.
2. Compare the legal forms of business enterprise.
3. Explain plans for getting the work done.
4. Identify problems unique to the family-owned business.
5. Describe sources of assistance for planning the enterprise.
6. Identify the role models and support systems for entrepreneurs.

ENTREPRENEUR PROFILE Steve Jobs & Steve Wozniak

Among the pioneers of the personal computer industry were Steven Jobs (top photo) and Stephen Wozniak, two friends who became business partners and founded Apple Computer, Inc. While he was still a junior high school student, Jobs met and befriended Wozniak, who was a few years older. Growing up in the area south of San Francisco that was home to major electronics companies, the two youths tinkered with electronic gadgets in their spare time. Parts and advice for their hobby were obtained from engineers in nearby high-tech firms. In 1976, when Jobs was in his early twenties and Wozniak was in his mid-twenties, the two partners were assembling computers in a garage for their friends in a computer club. These early computers, crude by today's standards, were slow and had little memory capacity.

The big breakthrough for Jobs and Wozniak came in 1976 when they received an order for fifty computers from one of the country's first computer stores, the Byte Shop in Mountain View, California. The two Steves lacked the money to buy parts and supplies to build the computers needed to fill the order. Jobs talked suppliers into selling to them on credit. Jobs sold his Volkswagen and Wozniak sold his two Hewlett-Packard calculators to raise $1,300 to open a primitive production line. Eventually, 600 units of this computer, the Apple I, were sold. Profits were used to start work on an improved model, the enormously successful

Apple II, which was introduced in 1977, the year Apple Computer, Inc., was formed. With a typewriter-style keyboard, video terminal, disk drive, and power supply, the Apple II was a major improvement over the previous model. Two competing computers, the Commodore Pet and the Tandy TRS-80, also entered the market in 1977.

Other than their mutual fascination for computers, Jobs and Wozniak seemed to have little in common. Jobs had always wanted to start a business and was competitive by nature. Wozniak, on the other hand, was the brilliant-scientist type and was not competitive. Their respective personalities, strengths, and skills seemed to complement each other. According to some industry observers, Wozniak created the first Apple computer while Jobs created the company to manufacture and sell it.

Jobs showed his aptitude for business and making money at an early age. For example, he earned spending money by fixing old stereo systems and selling them to his high school classmates. His knack for business continued at Apple Computer, where he watched over every detail of the business. He handled the advertising and public relations activities and also dealt with suppliers, customers, and prospective investors and lenders.

Apple Computer, Inc., is a success by almost any measure. The Apple II was easy to use, attractively designed, and came with accurate and concise operating manuals. More than 130,000 Apple II units had been sold by 1980. In addition, the company's sales volume increased from $800,000 in 1977 to $200 million in 1980.

There was no question that Apple was the dominant name in personal computers in 1980 with 80 percent of the market. The company had been doing everything right, or so it seemed. Then the company's good fortune began to change in two ways: its new computer model was a failure and IBM entered the market with a competing product.

After much fanfare, the Apple III was introduced at the National Computer Conference in 1980. After some short-lived early success, 14,000 units had to be recalled to remedy serious problems. Industry observers said the company had been lax about testing components and completed units. Then, in 1981, IBM announced that it was entering the personal computer market. Rather than being intimidated, Jobs placed a full-page advertisement in the *Wall Street Journal* with the headline: "WELCOME IBM. SERIOUSLY."

By 1983, Steve Wozniak had left the company to pursue other interests, and Steve Jobs had hired John Sculley from Pepsi to serve as president of Apple Computer, Inc. Following a power struggle within the company, Steve Jobs left Apple in 1985 and, shortly thereafter, founded a new company, Next, Inc. The first computer manufactured by this new company was a stylish-looking black cube with an oversized video screen, stereo sound, and a considerable amount of computing power and memory.

Source: Robert Levering, Michael Katz, and Milton Moskowitz, The Computer Entrepreneurs *(New York: NAL Books, 1984); Lee Butcher,* Accidental Millionaire *(New York: Paragon House Publishers, 1988); and Kenneth Morris, Marc Robinson, and Richard Kroll,* American Dreams: One Hundred Years of Business Ideas and Innovation from The Wall Street Journal *(New York: Lightbulb Press, 1990).*

DEFINITION OF THE BUSINESS

Your first step in starting a business is to turn your idea for a business into a plan of action. You will do this by writing a business plan. A business plan is a written description of every part of the new enterprise. Beginning with a definition of the business you intend to conduct, you will map out the course for the enterprise.

A definition of the business contains a description of the industry, your company, the products or services you will offer, and the image you desire.

THE INDUSTRY

All the firms that offer a particular product or service make up an ***industry***. IBM, Apple Computer, and the other computer manufacturers make up the computer industry. Likewise, PepsiCo, Inc., and Coca-Cola Company are two of the companies in the soft-drink industry. If you construct single-family houses, you are a part of the home building industry.

A definition of the business should include the outlook for the industry. Discuss changes or trends that could affect your business either positively or negatively. Are people buying more or less of the industry's product? Will new products from another industry make it harder or easier to sell your products?

YOUR COMPANY

A definition of the business must contain a description of the company you intend to start. Here is an example of a definition of a company:

> The store will sell a complete line of office supplies and custom-printed forms to consumers and to businesses. No other local firm offers such an extensive line of products. Offices, banks, and other business users will be given both discounted prices and free delivery service when they place large orders.

The business name is a part of the description of your company. You should explain the business name in the business plan. Because the name may be difficult to change later on, take care in selecting the name in the beginning. Your answers to the following questions should be helpful when deciding on a business name:

1. Does the name tell people what my company makes or sells?
2. Is any other company or organization using the name I am considering? Is anybody using a similar name? Two or more companies using the same or similar names can be confusing to customers. You may also find yourself in legal difficulty if you use an established firm's name.
3. Am I aware of the problems that may arise when I put my own name on the business? Having your name on the business could be embarrassing to you and your family if the business fails. On the other hand, if the business is successful, you may have difficulty selling it

because prospective buyers may not want a business with someone else's name on it. If you are successful in selling it, you may not like what the new owner does to your name through dishonesty or poor treatment of customers.

4. Is my company's name linked to a current fad, catchword, or anything else that could lose its popularity? If so, the name may someday tell customers that the business, along with its products and services, is outdated.

PRODUCTS AND SERVICES OFFERED

You can look at products and services from two different viewpoints: the seller's and the consumer's.

SELLER'S VIEWPOINT. The ***seller's viewpoint*** is a narrow definition of products and services. That is, many sellers see products as physical objects only. They think of the products in terms of the component parts and materials used in manufacturing. In a similar way, sellers may see services as consisting only of the tasks performed.

CONSUMER'S VIEWPOINT. From the ***consumer's viewpoint,*** products and services are seen in terms of the benefits derived from their use. The key idea is that consumers buy what the products or services will do for them. Therefore, entrepreneurs should see themselves as sellers of benefits. Consumers shopping for a microwave oven are buying more than just an oven. They are buying convenience and the ability to get meals on the table quickly. When you buy a car, you are probably buying more than a means of transportation. You may also be buying a symbol of status, taste, and achievement.

How will you answer the question, "What is your business?" Some examples may help you think of a response. The owner of a tire store may answer, "I sell more than tires, I sell customer safety." The operator of a fast-food restaurant may say, "I sell more than food, I sell family fun and convenience at a low price."

Illustration 5-1
For most people, a car is more than just a means of transportation.

IMAGE DESIRED

An enterprise can also be described in terms of its ***image,*** which is how customers feel about doing business with the enterprise. It is a personality and identity that makes customers think immediately of the business when they want the particular kind of products or services it offers. What makes or creates the image of a business? Image is the result of the total business and all its parts. You will determine the image when you (1) plan to sell specific products and services, (2) plan what customer services to offer, (3) select a location, and (4) hire employees.

SPECIFIC PRODUCTS AND SERVICES. After you select the type of enterprise you want, you must choose specific products and services to offer. You must define exactly what you are going to sell.

It is not enough to say that you will open an auto parts store. What parts will you keep in stock? Will you specialize in certain types of cars? Answers to these questions will help determine the image. If you stock parts for American-made cars, you will have one image. If you limit your inventory to parts for imported cars, you will have another image. You will have a third type of image if you specialize in parts for antique and restored cars.

You will have to make similar decisions if you open a service enterprise. As an example, the policy of one photographer might be to serve people who want pictures taken at weddings, family reunions, and other special occasions. Another photographer's services might be limited to taking portraits in the studio. In a similar way, owners of travel agencies, motels, and movie theaters must define exactly what services they sell.

CUSTOMER SERVICES. ***Customer services*** are the extra benefits that a business provides for its customers. For example, some grocery stores provide custom trimming of meat at no extra cost, neighborhood bulletin boards, and a courtesy booth for the payment of utility bills. Another example is clothing stores that offer free alterations on clothing purchased there.

Customer services are often associated with, but not limited to, retail stores. Think of the mail-order firms that permit a thirty-day trial of merchandise, the muffler shops that guarantee their product for as long as you own the car, and dry cleaners that offer one-hour service.

You must make definite plans about the customer services that you'll offer. Your decision will affect the image of the enterprise.

LOCATION. Where will the enterprise be located? A jeweler who wants to convey a quality image should locate near fashionable stores. On the other hand, a building materials discount store could be appropriately located in a warehouse district. In addition, customers should have easy access to the business with ample and convenient parking. When selecting a location, ask yourself this question: How will my customers feel about coming to this location?

EMPLOYEES. The attitude of employees affects the image of the business. A restaurant with excellent food will acquire a poor image if meals are not served promptly and courteously. An efficient appliance repair service may lose its clientele if employees are not polite when entering customers' homes.

You may be the only employee in the beginning. When you are ready to hire others, remember what image you want to establish for the enterprise. Then, hire only those employees who will help you achieve that image.

LEGAL FORMS OF BUSINESS ENTERPRISE

The three principal legal forms of business enterprise are (1) sole proprietorship, (2) partnership, and (3) corporation. One of the entrepreneur's most important decisions is choosing the appropriate legal form for the business. Before making this decision, prospective entrepreneurs should consider these questions:

1. How soon do I want to get the enterprise started?
2. Am I willing to share the profits with others?
3. Do I want complete control in running the enterprise?
4. How much liability am I willing and able to assume?
5. Will one particular legal form of business enterprise result in lower taxes?
6. Am I able to provide all the capital needed to get the enterprise started?
7. Is my enterprise based on a secret process or formula?
8. Do I want the enterprise to continue when I am no longer able to run it myself?

The legal form of organization affects most areas of the enterprise. Therefore, the entrepreneur should understand all three forms and be familiar with the advantages and disadvantages of each. At the same time, entrepreneurs should know they may be required to comply with certain regulations, regardless of the legal form of the enterprise. For example, the law generally requires every business with one or more employees to obtain an Employer Identification Number. Required on employers' tax returns, an Employer Identification Number is obtained by filing Form SS-4 with the Internal Revenue Service. This identification number is not the same as the Social Security number required on individual income tax returns.

An entrepreneur should also realize that the legal form of the business can be changed as the enterprise develops and grows. For instance, a new business may begin as a sole proprietorship and develop into a partnership. Some proprietorships and partnerships may later become corporations.

SOLE PROPRIETORSHIP

A ***sole proprietorship*** is an enterprise owned by only one person. It is sometimes referred to simply as a proprietorship. This is by far the most popular legal form of business enterprise. As shown in Figure 5-1, proprietorships greatly outnumber the two other legal forms. Proprietorships exist in just about every field of business activity. However, they are dominant in the areas of services, retail trade, and construction. Proprietorships generally have small sales volumes and employ only a few workers.

Figure 5-1
Number of Businesses in the United States (in thousands)

Industry	Sole Proprietorships	Partnerships	Corporations
Agriculture, forestry, and fishing	361	149	117
Mining	159	60	42
Construction	1,636	62	371
Manufacturing	360	35	294
Transportation, public utilities	648	30	148
Wholesale trade	339	20	317
Retail trade	1,974	165	650
Finance, insurance, and real estate	1,225	828	521
Services	5,977	291	1,120
TOTAL	12,679	1,640	3,580

Source: U.S. Bureau of the Census, Statistical Abstract of the United States: 1991, *111th ed. (Washington, DC: U.S. Government Printing Office, 1991), 525.*

ADVANTAGES OF SOLE PROPRIETORSHIP. Proprietorships are popular because of several advantages: (1) profits to owner, (2) easy start-up, (3) complete control and flexibility, (4) tax benefits, (5) satisfaction, (6) secrecy, and (7) easy dissolution.

Profits to Owner. A proprietor owns the business. A proprietor is the sole owner of any profits earned and does not have to share them with anyone else. This is not the case with other legal forms. In partnerships and corporations, some portion of the profits will be distributed to others.

Easy Start-up. Many people prefer the proprietorship because it is the easiest and simplest form of business to start. Generally, no legal document is necessary to establish a sole proprietorship. It exists as soon as business is conducted. For example, you can be the proprietor of your own carpet cleaning service as soon as you purchase the appropriate equipment and cleaning supplies. In other words, you could be in business and ready to serve your first customer by tomorrow.

Depending on the type of enterprise you open, you may have to obtain a license. For example, restaurants must usually be approved by the local board of health.

Complete Control and Flexibility. Since a sole proprietor does not have to get anyone else's approval, decisions affecting the business can usually be made more quickly. In partnerships and corporations, important decisions are generally made only after consulting others.

Consider a painting contractor who has an opportunity to buy paint at a bargain price. The order must be for a large quantity, and the order must be placed by the end of the day. In a sole proprietorship, the entrepreneur could make the decision in a matter of minutes. In a partnership or corporation, the entrepreneur might not be able to consult with the others by the deadline. As a result, the chance to save money would be lost.

Tax Benefits. Sole proprietors are taxed as individuals; the business itself is not taxed. Special taxes that are levied against a corporation do not apply to proprietorships.

The proprietorship's tax return is similar to any other individual taxpayer's. Personal and family deductions and exemptions are listed on the Internal Revenue Service Form 1040. In addition, proprietors file Schedule C to deduct business expenses from business income. ***Business income*** is total dollars received for all goods and services sold during the year. ***Business expenses*** are ordinary and necessary costs of operating the business. Generally, a sole proprietor may deduct expenses such as employees' wages and salaries, interest on business debts, insurance premiums, bad debts, and rent on buildings, trucks, and other equipment.

Satisfaction. The proprietor of a successful business enjoys a sense of accomplishment by applying skills, making personal sacrifices, and making decisions that often overcome obstacles. The satisfaction of knowing that one is largely responsible for the success of the enterprise is a reward in itself. If this reward must be shared with others, as in the other legal forms, the same feeling of satisfaction may not result.

Secrecy. Sole proprietorship offers the best possibility for keeping information confidential. This may be important if the success of the enterprise depends on a secret process or formula. Also, the owner does not have to tell anyone other than the Internal Revenue Service what the profits are.

Easy Dissolution. Proprietorships are easy to start, and they are almost as easy to dissolve. All a proprietor must do is sell the equipment, inventory, and other assets used in the enterprise. To protect the credit rating, a proprietor should make sure employees and creditors are paid in full.

DISADVANTAGES OF SOLE PROPRIETORSHIP. Sole proprietorships have these disadvantages: (1) unlimited liability, (2) limited life, (3) difficulty in obtaining capital, (4) management difficulty, and (5) little incentive for employees.

Unlimited Liability. Proprietors may keep all the profits of their businesses, but they also have unlimited liability. ***Unlimited liability*** means that they are personally liable for all business debts. A proprietor may have to use personal savings, investments, or belongings to settle debts. Therefore, proprietors risk not only their invested business capital but also their personal assets.

Limited Life. A proprietorship has limited life because it is directly tied to the life of the owner. ***Limited life*** means that the business will be dissolved upon the death, imprisonment, or bankruptcy of the proprietor. In addition, an extended illness or physical disability may force the owner to close the business. This poses problems for a family member or other heir wanting to continue the business. Instead of continuing the former enterprise, a new sole proprietorship would have to be established.

Difficulty in Obtaining Capital. Sole proprietors have two sources of funds for starting the business. One source is their own personal funds, which may not be adequate. The other source is borrowed funds. However, lenders often hesitate to grant loans to sole proprietors because of the risk involved in a new enterprise. Having insufficient operating funds can severely limit the enterprise's growth and may cause it to fail.

Management Difficulty. ***Management difficulty*** occurs because the proprietor carries the entire burden of managing the business. Some entrepreneurs describe this situation as "spreading themselves too thin." Someone must make the products, help customers, complete tax forms, write advertisements, collect overdue bills, and order merchandise. One person seldom does all these things equally well, but usually it is the proprietor who must do them alone. Spending time on these necessary tasks leaves less time for planning the future.

Little Incentive for Employees. By definition, a proprietorship does not have partners or part owners. Therefore, employees can never be more than employees. They cannot buy, or be given, a share of the ownership. This may cause a highly competent employee to quit and possibly even start a competing business.

PARTNERSHIP

A ***partnership*** is a business enterprise owned by two or more persons. This legal form of ownership overcomes some of the limitations of sole proprietorships. The name of the business often indicates a partnership: for example, Smith and Jones's Hardware or Bill and Tom's TV Repair. Several types of partnership arrangements exist. However, the following discussion deals with the more common type known as a general partnership. All partners in a ***general partnership*** have unlimited liability for the enterprise's debts.

ADVANTAGES OF PARTNERSHIP. Partnerships usually have these advantages: (1) easy start-up, (2) added capital, (3) combined management skills, (4) tax benefits, and (5) employee incentives.

Illustration 5-2
Going into business with a partner offers many advantages.

© Walter Hodges/Westlight

Easy Start-up. A partnership is almost as easy to form as a proprietorship. The enterprise is ready to start once the partners have agreed on various details about the partnership. For example, they must decide how much money each will invest, how profits and losses will be shared, and how assets will be divided if the business is dissolved. These and other important points should be included in a written agreement known as ***articles of partnership.*** This agreement is not required by law, but its use can prevent misunderstandings and legal difficulties. The following points are usually included in articles of partnership:

1. Name and location of the business
2. Names of partners
3. Date on which the partnership is formed
4. Scope of the business
5. Duration of the agreement
6. Amount of each partner's financial contribution
7. Description of how profits and losses are to be distributed
8. Compensation of partners
9. Duties and responsibilities of each partner
10. Description of how disputes will be resolved
11. Procedures for dissolving the partnership
12. Description of how net assets will be distributed if the partnership is dissolved

Added Capital. Many partnerships are formed because two or more people can assemble more money than one person can. This makes it possible to start a larger business and have reserve funds for unexpected expenses. Also, lenders may be more willing to grant loans because there is more than one person available to repay the debt.

Combined Management Skills. Each partner can contribute a skill to the enterprise that the other may not have. One partner may be an outstanding chef. The other may be a skilled manager who likes to keep records and supervise employees. By combining their skills, the two partners could open a restaurant. Together in a partnership they could be successful; working alone each might fail.

Tax Benefits. The partnership itself is not taxed. Instead, partners pay income tax on their individual portions of the enterprise's profits.

Employee Incentives. Partners can encourage competent employees to remain with the business by inviting them to become partners. Articles of partnership should be modified to reflect any changes.

DISADVANTAGES OF PARTNERSHIP. The strong points of the partnership may be overshadowed by one or more of the following disadvantages: (1) unlimited liability of the partners, (2) limited life, (3) divided authority, and (4) frozen investment.

Unlimited Liability of the Partners. Each partner is liable for all partnership debts. That is, creditors may sue any of the partners to settle the debt. This is true even if one partner has incurred the debt on behalf of the business.

Limited Life. The life of a partnership is limited and uncertain. Any change among the partners can cause the partnership to dissolve. The death or withdrawal of one partner will bring the enterprise to an end. However, the remaining partners may start a new partnership. Of course, this assumes they have enough money to buy the former partner's share of ownership.

Divided Authority. Because authority is shared by all partners, there is potential for disagreement. Each partner could have different ideas about hiring employees, buying merchandise, or advertising and sales promotion programs. Many otherwise successful enterprises have been dissolved because partners could not work together. The possibility that problems will occur increases with the number of partners.

Frozen Investment. It is often difficult to withdraw a partner's investment from a partnership. Even if the other partners are willing to buy one partner's share, the partners may struggle to agree on a fair price. Therefore, when going into a partnership, entrepreneurs should invest only those funds they can live without for a while.

CORPORATION

A ***corporation*** is an enterprise that has the legal rights, duties, and powers of a person. Because a corporation exists independently of its owners, a corporation is an artificial being or "person." A corporation may own property in its own name and may also enter into contracts, borrow money, and perform other day-to-day business activities.

Corporations are established by obtaining a charter from the state in which the business is to be located. The ***charter*** is a written document outlining the conditions under which the corporation will operate. The owners are called ***stockholders.*** Individuals become owners by buying shares of ***stock,*** which represent shares of ownership in the corporation. Some large corporations have thousands of stockholders, representing people from a variety of occupations. Generally, these people are interested in the business only as an investment. However, in small enterprises, the stockholders and the managers are the same individuals. To them, the business is more than an investment; the business represents their careers.

ADVANTAGES OF CORPORATION. Corporations are often thought of as large businesses. However, because of the advantages, many entrepreneurs have chosen this form of ownership for their enterprises. The main advantages are (1) limited liability, (2) continuous life, (3) easy transfer of ownership, (4) ability to attract funds, and (5) specialized management.

Limited Liability. In a corporation, the most a stockholder can lose is the amount of money invested in the business. Because a corporation is a separate entity, the corporation, rather than the owners, owes the debts. Therefore, personal savings and belongings will not be taken to pay debts of the corporation. This is a major advantage of the corporate form of ownership.

Continuous Life. When a proprietor or a partner dies, the business is ended legally. This is not true of corporations. A corporation's existence is not affected by the death or incapacity of an owner. The enterprise can operate indefinitely as long as it is profitable.

Easy Transfer of Ownership. Ownership in a proprietorship or partnership may be difficult to transfer to another person. This usually involves closing the enterprise and reorganizing it. In a corporation, however, stockholders can sell their stock to another person.

Ability to Attract Funds. Corporations are able to acquire additional funds by selling shares of stock. Individuals may be more willing to invest in corporations than in partnerships because their liability is limited. For these reasons, corporations usually have more opportunities to expand. They are able to get money for new buildings, equipment, and inventories.

Specialized Management. Proprietors and partners must perform a wide variety of functions. However, because they are frequently larger than other legal forms of business enterprise, corporations can have ***specialized management.*** This means that each person can concentrate on one set of duties. One manager may oversee the manufacturing of the product while another specializes in accounting.

DISADVANTAGES OF CORPORATION. The disadvantages of the corporate form of ownership are (1) complicated formation, (2) double taxation, (3) government regulation, (4) charter restrictions, and (5) little secrecy.

Complicated Formation. Getting a corporation started usually requires more time and money than other legal forms of ownership. For example, the corporation must conform to certain laws to obtain a charter from the state. Thus, a lawyer's services are needed in filing the necessary papers. In addition to the lawyer's fees, a corporation will probably have to pay a fee to the state.

Illustration 5-3
A lawyer's help is needed to handle the complications of forming a corporation.

Double Taxation. Perhaps the major disadvantage of the corporate form of ownership is the problem of ***double taxation.*** This means that profits are taxed twice. A corporation must pay taxes on its profits. Stockholders also have to pay personal income taxes on their share of the profits.

Government Regulation. Federal and state regulations of corporations have increased over the years. Depending on the state in which a corporation is chartered, various reports are required each year. The corporation must also register in all other states in which it does business. This often involves the payment of a special tax.

Charter Restrictions. A charter for a corporation indicates the type of business the corporation will pursue. The charter permits the enterprise to engage in only those business activities stated in the document. Therefore, a corporation cannot make a major change in its line of business until the charter is amended. This will take time and involve additional legal fees.

Little Secrecy. The more owners a corporation has, the more difficult it will be to maintain confidentiality. All stockholders are entitled to know sales, profit, and asset figures each year. A special production method may be impossible to keep secret.

ORGANIZATION OF THE ENTERPRISE

Planning how to get the work done is an important step in starting an enterprise. This involves deciding what tasks must be performed to make the enterprise a success. If there are other partners or employees, an entrepreneur must decide who will perform each task. An entrepreneur should also realize the importance of human resource management.

WHAT SKILLS ARE REQUIRED BY THE ENTERPRISE?

The first step in organizing the work of the enterprise is to determine what tasks should be performed. Some duties are necessary in almost all enterprises: making or buying products, providing services, setting prices, waiting on customers, paying bills, advertising, cleaning and maintenance, and preparing accounting and tax statements.

List every task that comes to mind. Do not worry about how small the task seems to be. Also, you need not follow a particular order or sequence. Just keep adding to the list until you believe it is complete.

WHO WILL PERFORM EACH TASK?

After identifying the necessary tasks for the enterprise, the entrepreneur should indicate who will perform each task. Do this with an organization chart. An ***organization chart*** is a diagram that shows how one job in the enterprise fits in with others. Of course, a one-person enterprise does not need an organization chart.

The organization chart should be on paper and explained to all members of the enterprise. Figure 5-2 shows an organization chart for a carry-out pizza shop. The lines show that the counterperson and the deliveryperson report to the owner.

Figure 5-2
Carry-out Pizza Shop Organization Chart

OWNER
Supervises employees
Buys ingredients
Plans advertising
Makes pizzas
Keeps records
Cleans the kitchen

COUNTERPERSON
Takes counter orders
Takes telephone orders
Collects money from customers
Cleans counter and serving area

DELIVERYPERSON
Delivers pizza to customer
Collects money from customers

Figure 5-3 is an example of an organization chart for a computer store. This organization chart shows how two partners could divide the duties in their computer store. One partner is the marketing manager responsible for hiring, training, and supervising all salespersons as well as buying merchandise, planning advertising, and keeping records. The other partner is the service manager responsible for hiring, training, and supervising repair technicians.

Figure 5-3
Computer Store Organization Chart

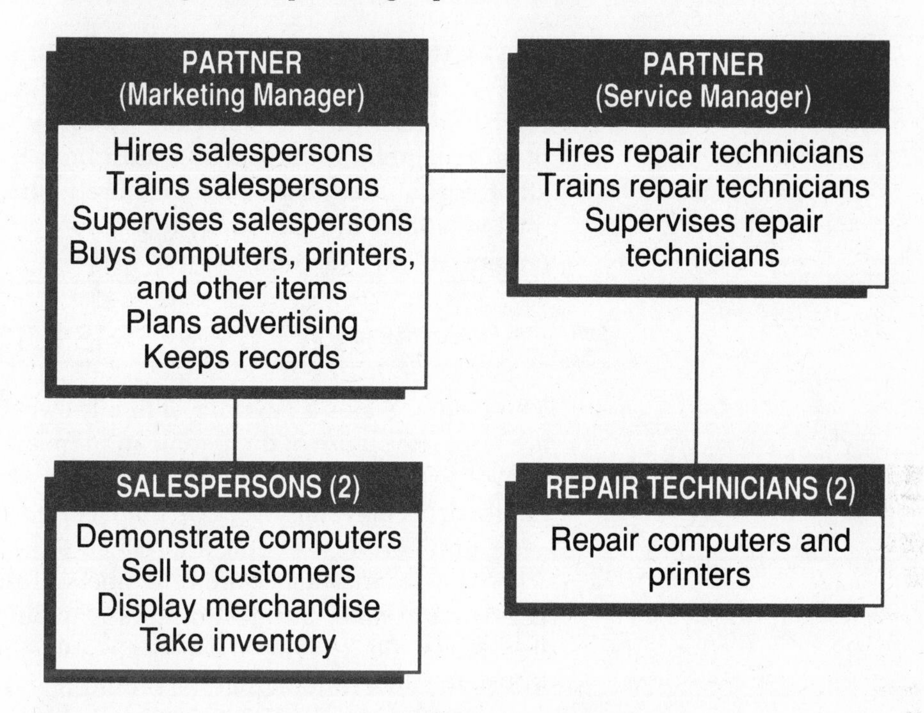

WHAT IS HUMAN RESOURCE MANAGEMENT?

The single most important resource in an enterprise is its people. Therefore, an entrepreneur must be prepared to manage this resource. The purpose of ***human resource management*** is to build a motivated and effective work force. The activities that make up this process are (1) hiring, (2) training, (3) determining compensation, and (4) determining employee benefits.

HIRING. The ***hiring*** process involves deciding whether a prospective employee is suitable for the job. Employers interview job applicants and also contact persons listed as references on the employment application form. As the firm grows in size, however, additional methods may be used. For example, persons applying for jobs may be required to take written tests or demonstrate that they can perform the work.

TRAINING. The purpose of ***training*** is to improve job performance. All new employees require a certain amount of training. Those without prior experience must be taught the skills to do the job. Employees with related job experience probably were hired because they have the skills. However, they still need training. For example, they may have to learn the procedure for handling customer complaints or making bank deposits.

DETERMINING COMPENSATION. ***Compensation*** refers to wages and salaries paid to employees. ***Wages*** are payments to workers on an hourly basis. ***Salaries*** are fixed dollar amounts paid regularly, such as weekly or monthly. Consider the following questions as you set your compensation policy: What are you willing to pay? What can you afford to pay? What must you pay to get the employees you want?

DETERMINING EMPLOYEE BENEFITS. Employees may receive ***employee benefits*** in addition to regular compensation. Entrepreneurs offer fringe benefits to compete effectively for good employees. A popular benefit today is health insurance, in which the employer pays all or part of the health insurance premium. Other fringe benefits are paid vacations and holidays, life insurance plans, and pensions. Some employees get a discount on purchases.

FAMILY-OWNED BUSINESS ISSUES

The United States is a nation of family-owned enterprises. These firms are unique because of the people in them and the relationship of those people to each other. Like people in every kind of firm, the people in family firms are employees or managers. At the same time, however, some or all of these people are related to each other.

Problems may arise when members of the family are also employees. For example, business owners may be torn when faced with the decision to fill a higher-paying or management position. Should the job go to a son or daughter, or should it go to an employee who is not a member of the family? And when a low sales volume leads to a reduction in the work force, there may be a reluctance to lay off members of the family.

A problem that may arise is rivalry among various parts of the family when the founder wishes to retire. Each of the sons or daughters may believe that he or she should be placed in charge of the business. The rivalry could destroy both the business and the family relationships. If agreement cannot be reached with family members, the owner may have to sell the business to outsiders.

A different type of problem results when a business owner learns that daughters or sons are not interested in making a career of running the business. Owners often prefer to pass their businesses on to the next generation. When that generation shows no interest in the opportunity, however, owners have no alternative but to sell to outsiders.

SOURCES OF ASSISTANCE

Starting a business is a complex process, regardless of whether you start from scratch, buy an existing business, or buy a franchise. As a prospective entrepreneur, you should obtain the assistance of advisers in business matters. Advisers you should contact include (1) attorneys, (2) accountants, (3) bankers, (4) trade associations, and (5) the Small Business Administration.

ATTORNEYS

Some persons visit an attorney only when they are involved in a lawsuit. However, many entrepreneurs have learned to consult an attorney on other matters as well. An attorney can help set up the business and give advance warning of potential legal problems. Compliance with local, state, and federal laws can be best assured with legal advice. An entrepreneur should study documents such as licenses, permits, and equipment purchase and lease agreements. When considering a franchise, a franchisee should examine carefully the contract used by the franchisor. Paying an attorney for these services is usually money well spent. If possible, select an attorney who is familiar with small business.

ACCOUNTANTS

Records of sales, expenses, and profits are necessary in managing an enterprise. Accountants can assist in setting up the records system to provide this information. They can also advise on tax problems and prepare tax returns. A prospective franchisee should discuss the franchisor's financial records with an accountant. With an accountant's help, a prospective franchisee can find out if the franchisor's estimates of sales and profits are realistic.

Illustration 5-4
Accountants help entrepreneurs set up recordkeeping systems and handle tax matters.

BANKERS

Although bankers are best known as lenders of money, they can also provide valuable information on starting a business. Bankers are able to do this because they keep in close touch with the business community. Bankers can help in comparing franchises or in checking credit ratings of customers. Although bankers are not experts in every area, they can usually help select other professional advisers. For example, they may give you the names of attorneys to consider.

TRADE ASSOCIATIONS

Another source of assistance is a trade association. A ***trade association*** is a group of businesses that have joined together to benefit a particular line of business. Examples are the National Restaurant Association, the Archery Lane Operators Association, and the National Auto Dealers Association. These groups assist members by offering ideas and information that will contribute to better management.

If you are interested in franchising, you should know about the International Franchise Association (IFA). This is an organization representing franchisors selling many types of products and services. Members must meet several requirements and adhere to a code of ethics. Because of these standards, IFA is seen as the spokesperson for responsible franchising. IFA booklets, including a list of members, may be available in your local library. You will also find extensive information in the Franchise Opportunities Handbook published by the U.S. Department of Commerce.

SMALL BUSINESS ADMINISTRATION

The Small Business Administration (SBA) is a government agency established to assist small businesses. The SBA helps small firms borrow money and operate more effectively. The SBA also offers management assistance directly to entrepreneurs. In addition, the SBA publishes a number of booklets on a variety of business topics. For SBA information, contact an office in your city or state or write the SBA, 1441 L Street, N.W., Washington, DC 20416.

ROLE MODELS AND SUPPORT SYSTEMS FOR ENTREPRENEURS

Role models, the persons we pattern our behavior after, are often important factors influencing entrepreneurs in their career choices. Parents, brothers, sisters, other relatives, friends, or acquaintances could all be your role models. People you know of only by reputation, such as successful entrepreneurs who have come to your attention in the mass media, could also be your role models. Some people look at the entrepreneurial accomplishments of their successful role models and say, "If they can start their own businesses and be successful, so can I."

In addition to role models, entrepreneurs also need personal networks—informal groups through which people obtain information and support. Two types of personal networks are moral support networks and professional support networks. Moral support networks consist of family members and friends who serve as a cheering squad, offering encouraging words during difficult times. Professional support networks can be a valuable source of the business and technical advice entrepreneurs need. Included in this network are other entrepreneurs, prospective customers, and suppliers who will be selling products and services to the new venture. Advisers such as attorneys and accountants could also be included in a professional support network.

ACTION STEPS FOR ASPIRING ENTREPRENEURS

Use these action steps to help you prepare for the possibility of being an entrepreneur at some point in your career:

1. Read about an industry in which you have an interest. Find out what it is that attracts you to this industry.
2. Start writing a definition of the business you would like to start. The process of writing down your ideas will help you sharpen your focus. Review the definition at least once a month and revise it as often as necessary.
3. Discuss the advantages and disadvantages of each of the legal forms of business enterprise with a lawyer.
4. Analyze yourself to determine your strengths and weaknesses. If you start your own business, you will need help from people who complement your skills.

BUILDING YOUR ENTERPRISE VOCABULARY

Match the following terms with the statements that best describe applications of those terms. Write the letter of your choice in the space provided.

a. industry
b. consumer's viewpoint
c. business expenses
d. limited life
e. general partnership
f. role models
g. double taxation
h. human resources management
i. employee benefits
j. organization chart

_______ 1. Wages paid to employees, insurance premiums, and rent on the building are examples.
_______ 2. Maria, Samantha, and the other owners are responsible for the firm's debts.
_______ 3. Offered to employees in addition to wages and salaries.
_______ 4. What your business and all other businesses offering the same product or service comprise.
_______ 5. Both the corporation and the stockholders pay taxes.
_______ 6. The business was dissolved when the owner died.
_______ 7. Shows who an employee is responsible to in the company.
_______ 8. Buying products or services because of the benefits they provide.
_______ 9. "Watching my aunt start a successful business has inspired me to become an entrepreneur."
_______ 10. Hiring and training are included.

UNDERSTANDING KEY CONCEPTS

Write a short answer to each of the questions below.

1. What should a definition of the business contain?

____

____

____

____

2. What is the first step in planning how to get the work done in the enterprise?

____

____

____

____

3. Describe two problems that may arise in a family-owned business.

4. List five types of advisers to contact when starting a new business.

5. What are the two types of personal networks for entrepreneurs?

6. Compare the three legal forms of business enterprise by writing the advantages and disadvantages of each in the spaces provided on the next page. Select your answers from the list below. Some terms will be used more than once.

easy start-up
difficulty in obtaining capital
complicated formation
easy transfer of ownership
owner profits
little incentive for employees
satisfaction
unlimited liability
little secrecy
frozen investment
limited liability
combined management skills
management difficulty
easy dissolution
limited life
double taxation
ability to attract funds
complete control and flexibility
employee incentives
divided authority
secrecy
continuous life
government regulation
added capital
charter restrictions
tax benefits
specialized management

Legal Forms of Business Enterprise	Advantages	Disadvantages
Sole Proprietorship		
Partnership		
Corporation		

APPLYING YOUR ENTERPRISE KNOWLEDGE

These activities will give you a chance to apply what you have learned in Chapter 5.

1. By completing the exercises below, you will gain experience in describing products and services from the consumer's viewpoint. For each enterprise listed, describe the benefits that consumers derive from its products or services. The first statement has been completed to help you get started.

ENTERPRISE #1: CRAFT AND HOBBY SHOP

Benefits of products or services: *The products permit consumers to engage in creative leisure-time activities.*

ENTERPRISE #2: VIDEO MOVIE RENTAL STORE

Benefits of products or services: ____________________

____

____

ENTERPRISE #3: PHOTOGRAPHY STUDIO

Benefits of products or services: ____________________

____

____

ENTERPRISE #4: AEROBICS AND FITNESS CENTER

Benefits of products or services: ____________________

____

____

ENTERPRISE #5: CLOTHING STORE

Benefits of products or services: ____________________

____

____

ENTERPRISE #6: MINIATURE GOLF COURSE

Benefits of products or services: ____________________

____

____

2. Why should partners develop articles of partnership?

____

____

____

____

3. What types of items should be included in articles of partnership?

____

____

____

____

____

____

4. In the space provided, draw an organization chart for the enterprises described below and on page 134.
   a. This enterprise is a proprietorship engaged in selling and installing solar water heaters. There are four employees in addition to the owner. The owner buys the solar water heaters and other supplies needed to operate the business. Two installers are responsible for installing the solar water heaters in customers' homes or businesses. One salesperson sells solar water heaters. A part-time secretary is responsible for preparing and mailing bills to customers and depositing money in the bank.

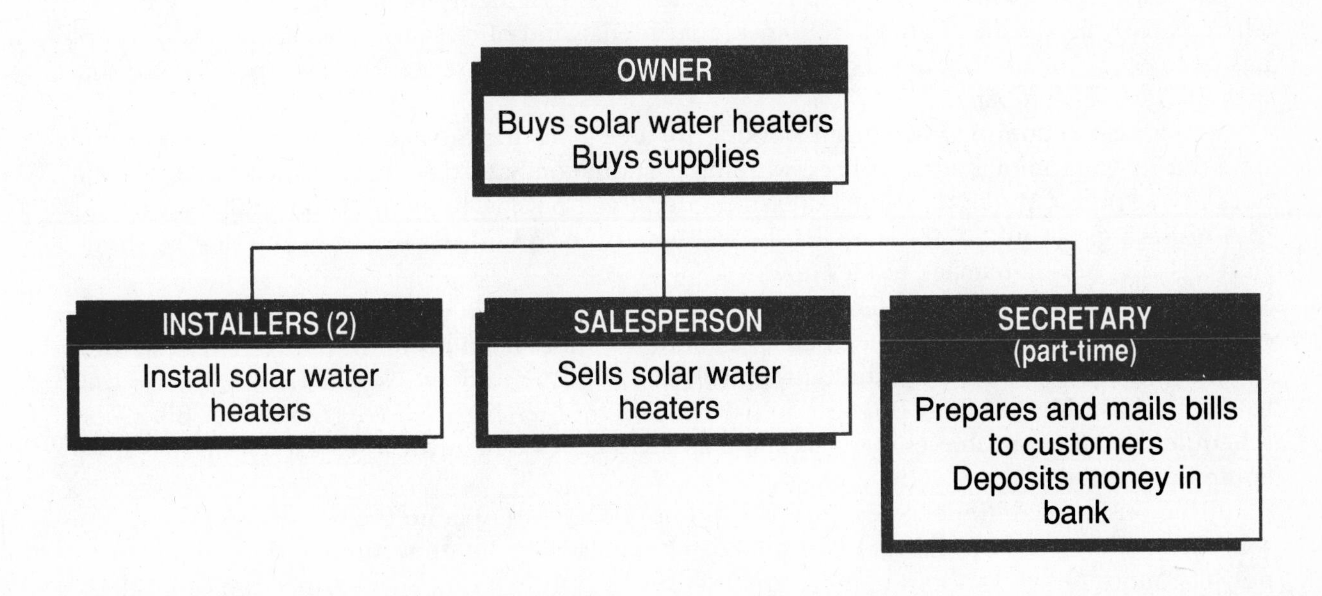

b. This enterprise provides maintenance and janitorial services for owners of office buildings. The business is operated by two partners. One partner is the business manager responsible for keeping records, contacting potential customers, and purchasing supplies and equipment. The other partner is the operations manager responsible for hiring, training, and supervising the five employees, who are all janitors. The janitors are responsible for mopping and waxing floors, vacuuming and shampooing carpets, washing windows, and emptying wastebaskets.

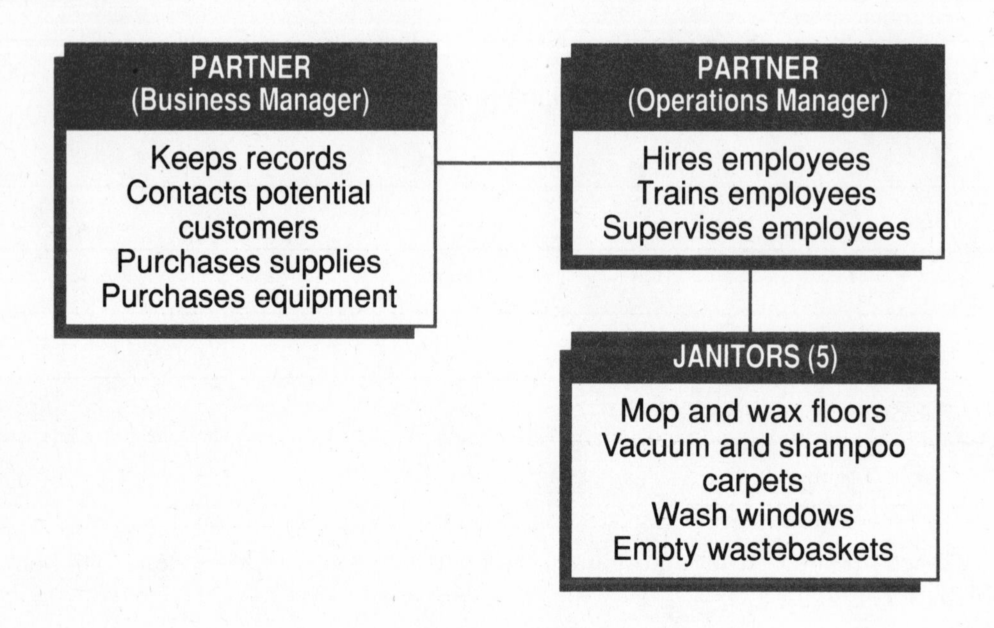

SOLVING BUSINESS PROBLEMS: LEE'S MOVING SERVICE

Ed Lee started Lee's Moving Service three years ago to supplement his earnings as a house painter. The company moves the contents of homes, apartments, and offices anywhere in the city. Business has been so good recently that Ed has stopped painting houses so that he can spend more time with the moving company.

Bill, a high school senior, started working for Lee's Moving Service last year. He worked full-time during the summer and has been working part-time on Saturdays, during the school year. Bill likes the work and the opportunity to earn money. Each payday, he deposits one-half his earnings into his savings account. Bill knows that he will have his own business someday and that he should start learning how to manage money now.

With graduation only a few months away, Bill is thinking about what he will be doing next year. He plans to enroll in the community college about five miles from his home. Until yesterday, when he talked to Ed Lee, Bill was planning to enroll as a full-time student. Now Bill doesn't know what to do. Ed has offered him a full-time job starting right after high school graduation. Bill's work schedule would be flexible enough to allow him to take one or two classes each semester at the community college.

If the business continues to expand, Ed will not be able to operate the moving service by himself. On several occasions, Ed said that someday Bill may have the opportunity to become his partner. The more he thinks about it, the more Bill likes the idea of being in a partnership with Ed.

1. Should Bill accept Ed's offer of a full-time job starting after graduation? Why or why not?

2. What would Ed gain by forming a partnership with Bill?

3. What would Bill gain by becoming Ed's partner?

4. Which of the three legal forms of business enterprise would you recommend for Lee's Moving Service? Why?

BUSINESS PLAN PROJECT

Use the space provided on pages 137 and 138 for the business plan activities below.

1. Write a definition of your business.
2. Describe the consumer benefits of your products or services.
3. List the customer services you will offer.
4. Indicate which legal form you have chosen for the enterprise. Then explain why you made that choice.
5. Indicate how many employees you will need. Make sure this agrees with the information you provided for the Business Plan Project activity in Chapter 3.
6. Draw an organization chart for your enterprise. Draw a box to represent each position and list the main job tasks in each box.

DEFINITION OF THE BUSINESS

BENEFITS OF PRODUCTS OR SERVICES

CUSTOMER SERVICES

LEGAL FORM

The legal form of organization for the enterprise is: ______________________________

Reasons for choosing this legal form are: ______________________________

____

____

NUMBER OF EMPLOYEES

The number of full-time employees is: ______________________________

The number of part-time employees is: ______________________________

ORGANIZATION CHART

OWNER/SALESPERSON
Buys inventory and supplies
Plans advertising
Hires, trains, and supervises employees
Sells athletic shoes

SALESPEOPLE (one full-time, two part-time)
Sell athletic shoes
Keep stockroom orderly
Take inventory counts

BOOKKEEPER (part-time)
Keeps records
Prepares bank deposits
Prepares financial statements

CHAPTER 6

MARKETING THE PRODUCT OR SERVICE

In your Business Plan Project activities in earlier chapters, you have described your business, the products or services you will offer, and your target market. Now you should consider how you will reach these potential customers.

Learning Objectives

After you have studied Chapter 6, you should be able to:

1. Define marketing.
2. Distinguish between consumer products and services and industrial products and services.
3. Describe the channels of distribution.
4. Explain methods of pricing products and services.
5. Discuss ways of promoting your products and services.
6. Identify factors that can influence and define ethical behavior.

ENTREPRENEUR PROFILE John H. Johnson

Black business pioneer John Johnson is chairman and chief executive officer of Johnson Publishing Company, Inc., the business he founded in 1942. The company, which is wholly owned by Johnson, is the leading publisher of black-oriented magazines. His company also owns three radio stations, a travel agency, a book publishing division, and a cosmetics division, and produces a syndicated TV series. Recently, Johnson Publishing and Spiegel, Inc., announced a joint venture to develop black women's fashions and a related mail-order business.

John Johnson is a wealthy man, but he did not start out in life that way. He was born on January 19, 1918, in a tin-roofed house near the Mississippi River levee in Arkansas City, Arkansas. His father worked in a sawmill and as a laborer on the levee. His mother worked as a domestic and as a cook. John's father died when he was 8 years old. The following year, his mother married James Williams, a bakery deliveryperson. John credits his mother, father, and stepfather with providing him with the values and motivation to succeed in life and to assume a leadership position in corporate America.

John learned how to work before he learned how to play. When other children his age were playing with their toys, he was hard at work helping his parents whenever he could. At an early age, he learned how to wash and iron clothes. He also learned how to cook and, while still in elementary school, prepared meals for as many as fifty men who were working on the levee.

At the age of 24, and while he was still attending college, John started his publishing business in Chicago. While holding a part-time job with the Supreme Liberty Life Insurance Company, he got the idea for a magazine oriented to blacks. One of the jobs assigned to him by Harry H. Pace, the company's president and chief executive officer, was to summarize news about the black community from magazines and newspapers. Pace, a well-known and successful black businessman, used the information to stay abreast of developments in race relations.

Gathering the information for Harry Pace made John one of the most knowledgeable people about the black community in Chicago. When he told his friends and acquaintances about what he had been reading, they often asked him where they could obtain copies of the articles he was discussing. Some people even offered to pay him just for telling them where various articles appeared. John soon realized that he could be successful publishing a digest of the information that he was now so skilled at collecting and summarizing.

John began mailing a $2 subscription offer to potential subscribers, all of whom had insurance policies with Supreme Liberty Life Insurance Company. With Harry Pace's permission, John would use the company's mailing list and blank stationery. When he applied for a bank loan to pay the postage, he was turned down. However, his mother agreed to help and pledged her new furniture as collateral for a $500 loan. The subscription offer was mailed to 20,000 people. John received 3,000 replies and used the $6,000 to print the first issue of *Negro Digest*. Circulation of this digest reached 50,000 by the end of that year. The starting point for business success, as John found out, was to look for ways to meet people's needs.

In 1945, Johnson started publishing *Ebony,* a magazine that focuses on black culture and achievements. The magazine became an instant hit. *Ebony,* and *Jet* magazine, which was introduced in 1951, were the only black-oriented magazines for the next two decades.

Having observed that *Ebony* fashion show models had to mix their own makeup to match their dark skin tones, and realizing that existing cosmetics firms were not serving this market, John decided to start his own cosmetics company. Fashion Fair Cosmetics was founded in 1973. This was yet another example of meeting people's needs.

With annual sales in excess of $250 million and more than 2,300 employees, Johnson Publishing is the largest black-oriented corporation and the second-largest black-owned business in America. John Johnson is not interested in retiring. In fact, he said, "Young or not, if I get a few more years, I'm going to create a bigger company despite age, despite race, despite the odds."

Source: John H. Johnson with Lerone Bennett, Jr., Succeeding Against the Odds *(New York: Warner Books, 1989), and Gary Hoover, Alta Campbell, and Patrick J. Spain, eds.,* Hoover's Handbook of American Business 1992 *(Austin, TX: The Reference Press, 1991), 328.*

MARKETING

Marketing is a set of business activities that provides products and services to satisfy consumer needs and wants. Marketing connects those who produce the product or service with those who use it. The methods you use in reaching the target market comprise your ***marketing strategy***.

The ***marketing concept*** is a way of thinking about a business in terms of consumer needs and wants. This concept is based on three basic beliefs:

1. An entrepreneur should plan the business activities of an enterprise with consumers in mind.
2. An entrepreneur should blend the marketing efforts to fit the target market.
3. An entrepreneur should pursue profit as one of the enterprise's goals.

In other words, entrepreneurs should be concerned with both consumers and profits.

Five elements of the marketing process are important to the new enterprise: (1) identifying the products or services that consumers need and want, (2) recognizing the differences between consumer products and services and industrial products and services, (3) selecting the path the product will follow from producers to users, (4) providing products or services at prices customers are able and willing to pay, and (5) informing and persuading people that the enterprise aims to serve them.

You have already identified the products or services that consumers need and want—the first element of the marketing process. You did this when you chose an idea for a new enterprise. The remaining elements of the marketing process will be discussed in this chapter.

TYPES OF PRODUCTS AND SERVICES

Products and services can be divided into two large groups: consumer products and services and industrial products and services. The marketing strategy you use will depend on the type of product or service you will provide.

CONSUMER PRODUCTS

Consumer products are products individuals and families buy for their personal use. Many U.S. consumers enjoy a level of income enabling them to buy many different products. This spending power allows many people to try new products as their needs and wants change. These changes, together with amazing advances in technology, stimulate a constant flow of consumer products both into and out of the marketplace. New products and improved versions of old products appear daily on the counters and shelves of retail stores. At the same time, other products disappear from the stores because they are no longer in demand.

Consumer products are classified as convenience goods, shopping goods, or specialty goods. These categories are based on the buying habits of consumers.

CONVENIENCE GOODS. Inexpensive items that consumers buy often and with little shopping effort are ***convenience goods.*** With goods in this category, the cost of comparing quality and price of similar items is greater than the benefits received. Shopping costs are measured in terms of both the time and money spent looking for a particular product.

Potato chips and milk are convenience goods. How much could you save, if anything, on these items by driving from store to store trying to find the lowest prices? If you find a lower price, how much lower is it likely to be? Would the savings be worth the time and gasoline used?

Disposable ballpoint pens, candy bars, and bread are other examples of convenience goods. Once you realize that your pen is running out of ink, you wish to buy a new one with the least possible trouble. You know exactly what you need and you want to buy a new pen without going a great distance.

A manufacturer of convenience goods will want to have the products available in as many locations as possible. Consumers do not wish to use much energy or effort to locate and buy these items. If these products are not widely available, manufacturers will lose sales to companies whose products are sold in convenient locations for customers.

SHOPPING GOODS. Items people buy after comparing the price, quality, and other features of similar items are ***shopping goods.*** With goods in this category, the benefits of comparing products are greater than the shopping costs. In other words, the time and money spent looking for a particular item are worth it. Often, consumers of shopping goods do not have a clear idea of what to buy. Instead, they wish to compare the offerings of several stores to help them decide what to buy and where to buy it. Examples of shopping goods are stereo equipment, microcomputers, automobiles, shoes, and clothing. Compared to convenience goods, shopping goods usually are more expensive and are bought less often.

If you plan to sell shopping goods, choose a location where customers can compare what you offer with that offered by other stores. You may have noticed that one furniture store is likely to be located near another furniture store. The same is true for new car dealerships. Also, the last time you walked through a large shopping mall, you probably saw several shoe stores. Generally stores selling similar shopping goods should be located near each other because consumers want it that way.

SPECIALTY GOODS. Products that consumers will make a special effort to buy are ***specialty goods.*** The attraction of specialty goods lies in the particular features that distinguish the goods from similar products. Consumers of specialty goods know what they want, and they do not wish to go to several stores comparing items. Prestige brands of clothing, household appliances, and stereo equipment are examples of products often purchased as specialty goods. Lesser-known brands of these types of products are usually shopping goods.

Specialty goods may or may not be higher-priced items. Brand preference is often the reason for the purchase. For example, some people like a particular brand of imported cheese so much that they will go to out-of-the-way stores to buy that brand.

Illustration 6-1
People are willing to make a special effort to find specialty goods.

Spencer Grant/Stock, Boston

A manufacturer of specialty goods should select one or only a few stores to sell the items in a given community. Because customers are willing to travel several miles to buy the product, the retail location is not a major factor in the successful marketing of specialty goods.

CONSUMER SERVICES

Consumer services are tasks individuals and families pay others to do or provide for them. Services are intangible; you cannot touch them. Examples of enterprises providing consumer services include travel agencies, day-care centers, hotels and motels, and video movie rental stores.

INDUSTRIAL PRODUCTS

Industrial products are products that one business buys from another business. The business buys the industrial goods to produce other products, to provide services, to resell, or to use in daily operations. These items are often bought in large quantities, and many are made according to special orders. Users of industrial products include extractive firms, manufacturers, wholesalers, retailers, and service enterprises. Examples of industrial products include wood and varnish used by cabinet shops, paper and ink used by printing companies, and word processing equipment used by law offices.

Industrial products are classified according to how they are used by the purchasing company. Three categories are (1) raw materials, processed materials, and parts; (2) supplies; and (3) installations and accessory equipment.

RAW MATERIALS, PROCESSED MATERIALS, AND PARTS. Products that are in their natural state when businesses buy them are called ***raw materials.*** Other than what is necessary to transport them, these materials have not been processed in any way. Some raw materials are harvested or removed from where they are found in nature. Examples are minerals, timber, and agricultural commodities such as fruits, vegetables, cotton, wheat, and raw milk.

Products that are produced by one business, but will be changed into another form by other businesses, are called ***processed materials.*** Because of processing, you cannot recognize these materials in the finished products you buy. For example, you do not see the individual ingredients in the bakery products you buy. Chemicals and plastics are other examples of processed materials.

Parts are items incorporated into a finished product with little or no change. Examples of parts include buttons and zippers used on clothing, and tires and batteries used on cars. As soon as these items arrive at the factory, the manufacturer can install them on the product which is to be sold.

SUPPLIES. Items that aid in a firm's operations but do not become a part of the finished product are ***supplies.*** Examples are lubricating oil, pens and pencils, stationery, and heating fuel. Other supplies used in day-to-day operations are cash register tape, microcomputer diskettes, and cleaning products.

INSTALLATIONS AND ACCESSORY EQUIPMENT. Major items used to produce a product or to provide a service are called ***installations.*** Compared to other categories of industrial products, installations have a long useful life. Examples include factory buildings and expensive pieces of equipment such as mainframe computers and large printing presses. Other items in this category are jet airplanes used by airlines, transmitting equipment used by radio and television stations, and generators used by electric power companies.

Accessory equipment is also used in operating a business, but its useful life is short compared to that of installations. Hand tools and small power tools used by mechanics, forklift trucks used by warehouse employees, and electric floor sweepers used in a shopping mall are all examples of accessory equipment.

INDUSTRIAL SERVICES

Industrial services, also called ***business services,*** are tasks one business pays another business to perform for it. Examples of enterprises providing these services are public accounting firms, advertising agencies, computer consultants, meeting planners, and agencies supplying temporary employees.

CHANNELS OF DISTRIBUTION

The path a product follows from the producer to consumers or business users is called a ***channel of distribution.*** Every extractive, manufacturing, wholesaling, retailing, and service enterprise is part of a channel of distribution. Businesses that aid in transferring goods from the producer to the user are called ***intermediaries.*** Intermediaries are often able to perform marketing activities, such as transporting and storing large quantities of goods, more efficiently than producers. Channels of distribution differ depending on whether they are for consumer products or for industrial products.

Services are not included in the following discussion of channels of distribution because intermediaries are not often used in the marketing of services. Services are produced and consumed at the same time. For example, a hairstylist performs the service while the customer sits in the chair. The channel of distribution for services, therefore, is direct from producer to consumer.

CHANNELS FOR CONSUMER PRODUCTS

As shown in Figure 6-1, five channels of distribution widely used in the marketing of consumer products are (1) producer–consumer, (2) producer–retailer–consumer, (3) producer–wholesaler–retailer–consumer, (4) producer–agent–retailer–consumer, and (5) producer–agent–wholesaler–retailer–consumer.

Figure 6-1
Channels of Distribution for Consumer Products

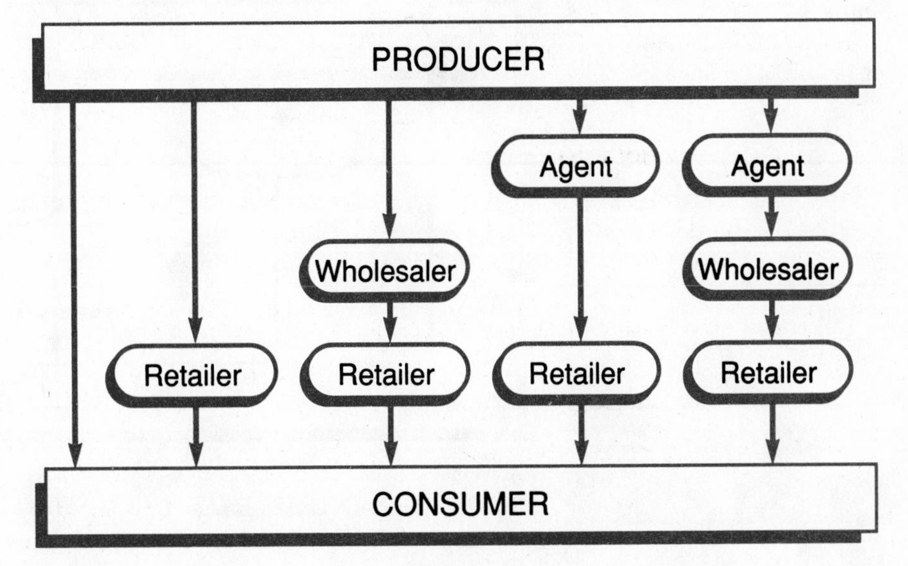

PRODUCER–CONSUMER. The shortest and simplest channel of distribution for consumer products is from the producer to the consumer. Producers sell door-to-door or by mail order.

PRODUCER–RETAILER–CONSUMER. Producers selling to large retail firms, such as the J. C. Penney Company or Sears, often use this channel. In addition, some manufacturers of paint, clothing, and other products have established their own retail stores.

PRODUCER–WHOLESALER–RETAILER–CONSUMER. This is the most common channel used by producers of convenience goods. Manufacturers with only a few products in their line cannot afford to personally contact the thousands of stores who sell the items. Instead, they sell through wholesalers. These wholesalers buy related products from many manufacturers and then sell an array of goods to retailers.

PRODUCER–AGENT–RETAILER–CONSUMER. Some producers sell to ***agents,*** who assist in the sale of products without owning the products. Agents bring buyers and sellers together. Sometimes agents work for manufacturers who are looking for stores to carry their products. At other times, they help retailers find sources of supply for certain goods.

PRODUCER–AGENT–WHOLESALER–RETAILER–CONSUMER. Producers often use this channel when selling to many wholesalers who are scattered throughout the country. Agents can be helpful in locating the wholesalers.

CHANNELS FOR INDUSTRIAL PRODUCTS

Four common channels of distribution for industrial products, as shown in Figure 6-2, are (1) producer–industrial user, (2) producer–agent–industrial user, (3) producer–industrial distributor–industrial user, and (4) producer–agent–industrial distributor–industrial user.

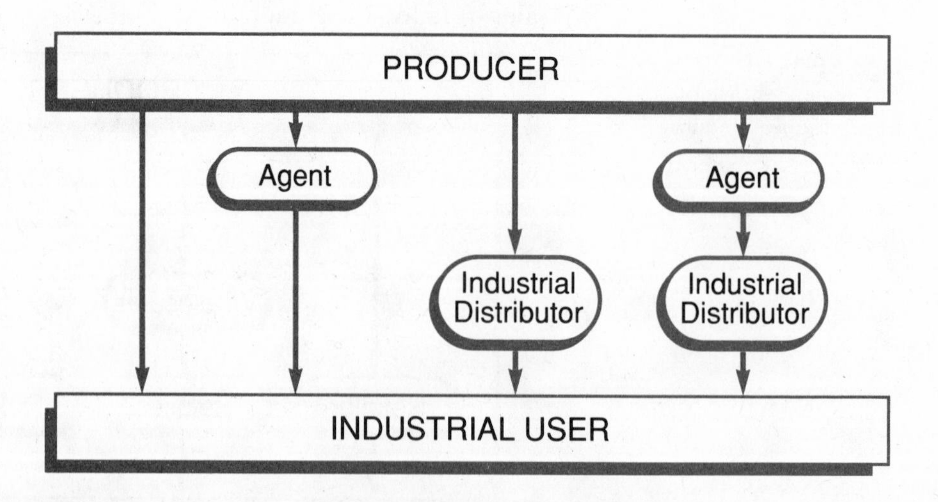

Figure 6-2
Channels of Distribution for Industrial Products

PRODUCER–INDUSTRIAL USER. This direct channel accounts for the largest dollar volume of industrial products sold. Manufacturers of installations, such as mainframe computers and large printing presses, usually sell directly to the users.

PRODUCER–AGENT–INDUSTRIAL USER. Some manufacturers do not employ their own salespeople. Instead, they rely on agents to locate buyers for their products. Companies having their own sales forces may use agents to sell a new product or to enter a new market.

PRODUCER–INDUSTRIAL DISTRIBUTOR–INDUSTRIAL USER. Some manufacturers find the services of industrial distributors helpful in reaching their customers. ***Industrial distributors*** are wholesalers who buy products from manufacturers and sell them to industrial users. They usually handle supplies and lower-priced accessory equipment.

PRODUCER–AGENT–INDUSTRIAL DISTRIBUTOR–INDUSTRIAL USER. This channel is used for inexpensive industrial products, particularly those that producers sell through many industrial distributors. Here, as is the case in consumer channels, agents bring buyers and sellers together. The producer is the seller and the industrial distributor is the buyer.

PRICING

What is price? ***Price*** is the exchange value of products and services stated in terms of money. Very simply, the price of a shirt is the amount of money required to buy the shirt. However, there is more to understanding price than merely finding out how much an item costs.

Manufacturers, wholesalers, retailers, and service enterprises use various methods of pricing products and services. Some pricing principles apply to all enterprises. In addition, each field of business has its own pricing practices. For example, extractive enterprises engage in diverse activities such as farming and commercial fishing. Therefore, specific pricing methods are difficult to identify. If you want to start an extractive enterprise, study pricing in the other fields of business. Then use those methods that best fit your enterprise.

Illustration 6-2
Businesses put a lot of thought into the price that the consumer sees.

COMMON PRICING PRINCIPLES

All entrepreneurs should be aware of three basic or common pricing principles: (1) all costs must be covered, (2) prices affect image, and (3) prices affect sales volume.

ALL COSTS MUST BE COVERED. No entrepreneur wants to stay in business unless enough money is received to cover costs and make a profit. Your price, then, must reflect the cost of goods or services; all expenses including employee wages, rent, and utilities; and some profit.

In manufacturing, the cost of goods sold is what it costs to make the product. In wholesaling and retailing, the cost of goods sold is what it costs to purchase the goods from others. In service enterprises, the cost of the service varies according to the amount of time and materials used.

PRICES AFFECT IMAGE. Prices charged usually result in a certain price image for the enterprise. Some firms try to give the image that they offer quality products or services at low or discount prices. This practice is successful in some instances and unsuccessful in others.

As an example, you may not hesitate to buy a radio with a well-known brand name at a low price. But would you go to a hairstylist whose prices were much lower than those of most others in town? If your answer is no, you probably believe that quality and price are related and that you should examine the quality when prices are low. Therefore, when setting prices, you should determine what your target market believes about how price and quality are related. This answer depends both on the person and on the specific product or service involved.

PRICES AFFECT SALES VOLUME. In many cases, as price increases, the amount of the product or service sold decreases. On the other hand, as price decreases, the amount sold increases.

As a result, you are faced with these three decisions:

1. Should you charge low prices and try to obtain more sales?
2. Should you charge high prices? The number of units sold would be lower, but the profit on each one would be higher.
3. Should you set prices somewhere between the low and high figures?

Here again, you must find out how each price would be accepted by the target market. Avoid the trial-and-error method of changing prices to see what happens to sales. This confuses customers and may damage your image.

PRICING BY MANUFACTURERS

The manufacturer's price must cover the cost of goods sold, all other costs, and a profit.

In a manufacturing enterprise, the cost of goods sold includes more than the cost of raw materials. It also includes the wages of factory workers and such costs as wear and tear on machinery. An entrepreneur must consider every item of cost before setting the prices.

PRICING BY WHOLESALERS

Wholesalers usually base their prices on the cost of goods sold plus a markup. ***Markup*** is the amount that is added to the cost of an item in arriving at the selling price. Markup, then, covers all the other costs plus a profit.

The cost of goods includes the cost of shipping the goods from the manufacturer to the wholesaler. Other major costs that must be covered by markup are rent, all wages and salaries, utilities, and delivery costs.

PRICING BY RETAILERS

Most retailers try to establish guidelines that help make pricing decisions simple and routine. This becomes more important as the number of items carried in stock increases.

Retail pricing is usually accomplished by taking a markup on cost. Using this method, the retailer adds a markup to the ***delivered cost of goods.*** The delivered cost of goods is the cost of the merchandise itself plus shipping costs. The markup method can be shown as follows:

Retail Price = Delivered Cost of Goods + Dollar Markup

Choosing the amount of markup is, of course, the important decision. If the overall store markup is too high, your products may be too expensive for your target market. As a result, you will lose customers to the competition. If the markup is too low, you may not be able to cover costs and earn a profit.

As a starting point, find out what the average markup percentage is for your line of retailing. Then adjust the rate to fit your situation as you learn more about your target market and your competitors.

Most retailers find it necessary to price some merchandise at other than average markup. You may decide to take a lower markup on some items to meet competitors' prices. On other items, you may take a higher markup because of customer services associated with them.

Markup is easy to calculate. For example, assume you paid $10 for an item, and you wish to take a 40 percent markup on it. Calculate the retail price as follows:

Cost × Markup Percentage = Dollar Markup
$10 × .40 = $4.00

Cost + Dollar Markup = Retail Price
$10 + $4 = $14

PRICING BY SERVICE ENTERPRISES

The service enterprise category includes a wide variety of businesses. Although the pricing methods vary among the service enterprises, many have one concept in common. This concept is that service firms generally charge an hourly fee for the number of hours spent in providing the service.

In addition to hourly fees, charges are made when materials, parts, or supplies are used. Repair businesses and the construction trades often use this approach to pricing.

Some service enterprises use specific charges for specific services. For instance, preparers of income tax returns usually charge a standard fee for completing a Form 1040. This is true no matter how long the preparer worked on the form. The price of a tune-up for a six-cylinder engine is the same even though it takes longer on some cars than others.

PRICING A NEW PRODUCT OR SERVICE

Deciding what to charge is not usually a problem when your product or service is the same as that of competitors. Whether they are buying consumer products or services or industrial products or services, customers will not often pay a price higher than that charged by other businesses. Entrepreneurs can match competitors' prices and then make sure they keep their costs down to where they can earn a profit.

Setting a price can be a problem, however, when introducing a new product or service. The practice of pricing according to what others charge will not work. An entrepreneur should use either a skimming pricing policy or a penetration pricing policy.

SKIMMING PRICING POLICY. With a ***skimming pricing policy,*** an entrepreneur would charge a relatively high price for the new product or service and expect to sell a low volume. The price would be high in relation to prices of comparable items. One purpose of this pricing policy is to try to recover as soon as possible the costs of developing the product. A disadvantage is that competitors will see a chance to make a profit from also selling the high-priced item. Realize that competition will eventually drive the price to a lower level. This is what happened to the prices of microwave ovens, pocket calculators, microcomputers, and videocassette recorders. An entrepreneur should also watch the sales of the product closely to see if the high price discourages customers from buying it.

PENETRATION PRICING POLICY. With a ***penetration pricing policy,*** the entrepreneur sets a low initial price to attract customers quickly. The lower price discourages other businesses from introducing the same product or service. An entrepreneur charges a low price and expects to sell a high volume of products or services.

PERSONAL SELLING, ADVERTISING, AND SALES PROMOTION

The final element of the marketing strategy is promotion. Through ***promotion,*** you inform customers of your offerings and persuade them to buy the products and services you have for sale. The two most widely used methods of promotion are personal selling and advertising. Another method is sales promotion, which is designed to supplement and coordinate personal selling and advertising.

PERSONAL SELLING

In ***personal selling,*** a salesperson makes direct contact with a customer. The purpose is to help customers buy the product or service that will fulfill their needs and wants.

The goal of a marketing strategy is to increase profitable sales. Personal selling is by far the major method of promotion used to reach this goal. Personal selling includes the activities of inside salespersons in retail, wholesale, and service enterprises. It also includes calls by outside salespersons on places of business as well as on consumers.

Illustration 6-3
A real estate agent is skilled at a specialized kind of selling.

A good personal selling program can give the new enterprise an advantage over larger competitors. Many businesses are too large to give the friendly, personal service that small enterprises can provide.

Three basic personal selling skills that you and your employees must develop are

1. The skill to determine the needs and wants of customers;
2. A solid foundation of product knowledge, including the product's uses, advantages, and limitations; and
3. The ability to convince customers that the product or service will fulfill their needs and wants.

ADVERTISING

Advertising is any nonpersonal presentation of information about products or services that is paid for by an identified sponsor.

The written or spoken words of an advertising message are contained in ***advertising copy.*** The ***media,*** such as newspapers, radio, magazines, and television, are the carriers of the advertising message. You should look for the most effective means to carry your message to your target market. Ask media representatives for information about their services and what results you can expect for your money.

The two types of advertising are product and institutional. ***Product advertising*** features specific products and services for the purpose of creating immediate sales volume. An advertisement for running shoes is an example. ***Institutional advertising*** focuses on the enterprise itself and is designed to create a favorable image and build goodwill. For example, a retail store may advertise that it offers many customer services.

Entrepreneurs may attempt to achieve the following goals through advertising:

- Encourage potential customers to visit stores or showrooms.
- Explain how products can be used.
- Announce the availability of parts or services.
- Invite requests for catalogs.
- Introduce new products or services.
- Explain new uses for old products.
- Encourage requests for samples of products.
- Depict the entrepreneur as a good citizen in the community.
- Explain product or service warranties.
- Announce locations where the enterprise's products or services may be purchased.

To plan an advertising program, you must identify the goals you want to achieve. Then, choose the messages and media that will help reach the goal.

Because you may not have much money to spend, try to get the maximum value for each dollar of advertising. To do this, you must first determine how much you will spend on advertising in the first year. Then check this against what similar enterprises spend. Trade associations usually have this information. In new enterprises, advertising expenditures are often slightly above average for the line of business. If the figure is too high, adjust it to fit your budget.

SALES PROMOTION

Sales promotion includes all those activities which are designed to build sales by supplementing advertising and personal selling. Sales promotion activities are directed toward your customers, whether they are individuals or other businesses.

Sales promotion activities designed for consumers include coupons, in-store product demonstrations, free samples, store counter and window displays, contests, and information booklets.

Various services that one business performs for another are a type of sales promotion. The purpose of these services is to encourage retailers or dealers to carry certain products. Examples include staffing booths at trade shows, offering free merchandise, conducting training programs for salespeople, installing displays, providing sales manuals, and furnishing other selling aids.

BUSINESS ETHICS

The public expects business people to conduct marketing and all other business activities in an ethical manner. ***Ethics*** is a set of rules that defines right and wrong conduct. By and large, business people support a concept of business ethics that is based on fairness, honesty, and adherence to the law. In addition, this concept suggests that entrepreneurs and managers should apply high standards of ethics when making business decisions. Nevertheless, there is always the possibility that what is considered to be ethical is not what is actually practiced. Three factors that influence and define ethical behavior are society, the law, and the stage of an individual's moral development.

SOCIETY

A large part of what is considered ethical behavior comes from the society in which the behavior occurs. Our society expects strict standards of ethical behavior in business. However, findings of various public opinion surveys indicate that citizens do not believe that those standards are always met and that they are dissatisfied with the level of ethical behavior. The demands and needs of society should eventually result in positive changes in ethical behavior by businesses and their owners and managers.

LAWS

Some of a society's ethical standards are expressed through court decisions and laws. ***Laws*** are values or standards of society that are enforceable through the courts. However, keep in mind that just because an action is legal does not necessarily mean it is ethical. In the past, for example, it was considered legal for managers of U.S. companies to discriminate against women and minorities in hiring and promotions. As the broader society recognized that these practices were unethical, laws were enacted in an attempt to stop them.

STAGES OF MORAL DEVELOPMENT

As individuals, we all have our own values and a sense of what is right and wrong. Further, some experts believe that people develop morally through a series of stages. At the lowest stage, people do the right things mainly to avoid punishment or to obtain approval. At the highest stage, a person's conduct is determined by his or her conscience and is based on ethical principles such as those related to justice, the equality of human rights, and respect for the dignity of individual human beings.

Illustration 6-4
It is no longer unusual to find a woman in a traditionally male occupation.

ACTION STEPS FOR ASPIRING ENTREPRENEURS

Use these action steps to help you prepare for the possibility of being an entrepreneur at some point in your career:

1. Go to businesses similar to the one you want to start, observe their operations, and determine the extent to which they follow the marketing concept.
2. Develop the skill of being able to look at different products and services and determining what customers are willing to pay for them.
3. Study how different companies promote their products and services and make a note of what you believe are the effective and ineffective methods used.
4. Learn enough about the businesses you come in contact with to determine if they meet society's standards of ethical behavior.

BUILDING YOUR ENTERPRISE VOCABULARY

Match the following terms with the statements that best describe applications of those terms. Write the letter of your choice in the space provided.

a. marketing
b. shopping goods
c. supplies
d. industrial services
e. agents
f. markup
g. skimming pricing policy
h. personal selling
i. media
j. ethics

_______ 1. Contacting a retailer to explain the benefits of your products.
_______ 2. A public accounting firm prepares financial statements for one of its business clients.
_______ 3. Concerned with satisfying consumer needs and wants.
_______ 4. Rules the public might use to judge the conduct of a business executive.
_______ 5. Are instrumental in bringing buyers and sellers together.
_______ 6. Competitors often locate near each other.
_______ 7. Magazines and television are examples.
_______ 8. Includes an amount equal to the planned profit.
_______ 9. Used up in the operation of the business.
_______ 10. One purpose is to recover product development costs.

UNDERSTANDING KEY CONCEPTS

Write a short answer to each of the following questions.

1. The marketing concept is based on three basic beliefs. List these.

____

____

____

2. What five elements of the marketing process are important to the new enterprise?

____

____

____

____

____

3. Products and services can be divided into what two large groups?

___

___

4. What five channels of distribution are widely used in the marketing of consumer products?

___

___

___

___

___

5. What is the meaning of the statement, "You should determine what your target market believes about how price and quality are related"?

___

___

___

___

___

___

___

6. List the three methods of promotion and give an example of each.

___

___

___

7. What are three factors that influence and define ethical behavior?

___

___

___

APPLYING YOUR ENTERPRISE KNOWLEDGE

These activities will give you a chance to apply what you have learned in Chapter 6.

1. Look at the advertisements for various products in one issue of a newspaper of your choice. Try to find advertisements for three products in each of these categories: convenience goods, shopping goods, and specialty goods. In the spaces below, list the products and tell whether you believe the store selling each one is located conveniently for you.

CONVENIENCE GOODS

____

____

____

____

SHOPPING GOODS

____

____

____

____

SPECIALTY GOODS

____

____

____

____

2. Contact a person who operates a business similar to the one you plan to start. Find out (1) from whom the majority of the products used in the business are bought, and (2) what businesses are included in the channel of distribution for the product.

   List the businesses from whom the majority of the products are bought. Then, on a separate sheet of paper, draw the channel of distribution for the products.

____

____

____

____

3. Ask five people to recall the last time they bought a product that had just been introduced. Then ask them whether they thought the price was high or low in relation to prices charged for comparable items. Summarize their answers in the space provided below.

	What was the product?	**Was the price high or low?**
Person #1		
Person #2		
Person #3		
Person #4		
Person #5		

4. Every day you are exposed to personal selling, advertising, and sales promotion. Based on your observations and your experience as a consumer, describe the promotional methods frequently used by the following enterprises. Some of the businesses that you are familiar with may not use all three promotional methods. The first item has been completed for you as an example.

BICYCLE SHOP

Personal Selling: *Bicycle features are explained to the customers; demonstration rides are available.*
Advertising: *Local newspaper advertising.*
Sales Promotion: *Some shops sponsor bicycle races.*

FAST-FOOD RESTAURANT

Personal Selling: ______________________

Advertising: ______________________

Sales Promotion: ______________________

PHOTO FINISHING SHOP

Personal Selling: ______________________________

____

Advertising: ______________________________

____

Sales Promotion: ______________________________

____

NEW CAR DEALER

Personal Selling: ______________________________

____

Advertising: ______________________________

____

Sales Promotion: ______________________________

____

What promotional methods are used by businesses similar to the one you plan to start?

Personal Selling: ______________________________

____

____

____

Advertising: ______________________________

____

____

Sales Promotion: ______________________________

____

____

SOLVING BUSINESS PROBLEMS: COMPLETE OFFICE SERVICES

Judy and Susan learned that many people earn a part or all of their income from businesses operated in their homes. In addition, many of these home-based entrepreneurs work alone. Additional help is often obtained from a spouse or other family member.

Examples of entrepreneurs operating businesses in their homes include mail-order retailers, real estate sales agents, distributors of gourmet foods, importers and exporters, advertising and public relations specialists, and bookkeepers. Regardless of the occupation or the line of trade, these people have similar concerns. Many worry about missing important telephone calls from potential customers. Others are concerned about the appearance of their typewritten letters and reports. Most also agree that they waste too much time waiting in line at the post office or the photocopy center. In short, they are frustrated at trying to operate a business and present a professional image without help.

Judy and Susan know that many home-based entrepreneurs need secretarial help but cannot afford to hire employees to perform routine office tasks. Judy and Susan are preparing to open Complete Office Services, an enterprise designed to serve the needs of people running businesses in their homes. Among the services they will offer are (1) telephone answering, (2) word processing, (3) photocopying, (4) maintaining mailing lists, and (5) organizing tax and financial records. Some of their customers may need all these services, while others may need only one service. In-home entrepreneurs will have access to professional-quality office services without adding more employees to their payrolls.

Judy and Susan know the costs of providing each of the services, but they have not decided how much to charge their customers. Since there is no other office services enterprise in the area to serve as a guide, they are searching for suggestions in setting their prices.

1. Should Judy and Susan set a price for each service and then charge every customer the same? Should they offer lower prices to those who buy a package of two or more services? Discuss the advantages and disadvantages of each method.

2. Should Judy and Susan use a skimming pricing policy or a penetration pricing policy? Explain the reasons for your recommendation.

3. In advertising the opening of Complete Office Services, should Judy and Susan list the prices for the various services? Give the reasons for your answer.

BUSINESS PLAN PROJECT

Use the space provided on pages 163 and 164 for the business plan activities below.

1. What companies supply the products you will use in your business? If there are too many to list, or if specific company names are not available, indicate the type of company; for example, auto parts wholesaler.
2. How will you decide what prices to charge? Indicate whether you will match competitors' prices, use a skimming pricing policy, or use a penetration pricing policy. Explain why you selected the particular pricing policy.
3. What promotional methods will you use at start-up and on a continuing basis? Describe how you will use personal selling, advertising, and sales promotion. Include any plans you have for placing advertising messages in newspapers or other media.

SUPPLIERS

Product	Name of Company

PRICING POLICY

PROMOTIONAL METHODS

	Promotional Methods to Be Used at Start-Up	Promotional Methods to Be Used on a Continual Basis
Personal Selling		
Advertising		
Sales Promotion		

CHAPTER 7

OBTAINING FINANCING

An entrepreneur needs money to start a business. In addition, he or she must be able to manage the money to ensure that the enterprise reaches its fullest potential. The term ***financing*** refers to the money and credit required to run a business. Some entrepreneurs go into business with the few dollars they have saved, only to find that this is not enough money. Unfortunately, they do not become aware of the problem until faced with a financial crisis, such as not being able to pay their employees or suppliers. Entrepreneurs should not expect to avoid all money problems. By anticipating their financial needs, however, entrepreneurs can plan ahead for the problems that may arise.

Learning Objectives

After you have studied Chapter 7, you should be able to:

1. Estimate start-up costs for a new enterprise.
2. Identify sources of funds.
3. Describe differences between short-term and long-term capital needs.
4. Identify needs for additional capital.
5. Suggest tips for requesting loans.

ENTREPRENEUR PROFILE Antonio R. Sanchez, Sr.

Antonio R. Sanchez, Sr., is a successful entrepreneur who heads the multimillion-dollar financial empire he founded more than thirty years ago in Laredo, Texas. The business success he and his son, who joined him as a partner, have enjoyed prompted *Forbes* magazine to predict that the Sanchez family might one day become known as a Mexican American dynasty.

A native of Webb County, Texas, Sanchez was born in 1916, the youngest of four children in a poor ranch family. He was a sickly child with severe asthma. Always ready to do whatever he needed to do to help himself, he took up boxing to expand his chest and lungs to try to counter the effects of the asthma. Sanchez was also always ready to help his family. As a child, he searched along the railroad tracks for coal spilled from passing trains to heat his family's home. Then, during the troubled economic times of the Great Depression, he dropped out of high school to help support his family.

Later, when Sanchez had a family of his own, he made his living selling and was described as an aggressive salesperson. He sold used cars and business machines and, for a time, owned his own small office supply company. His business success is attributed, at least in part, to the contacts he developed in and around Laredo. A number of those contacts were the result of his work in politics and his involvement in a political organization known as the Independent party.

In the early 1960s, Coastal States Producing Company wanted to hire someone from Laredo to scout properties and lease drilling rights in south Texas. Sanchez was hired for the job because of his thorough knowledge of the area. Always ambitious, Sanchez looked for ways to expand further into the oil business. Before long he had developed an active brokerage and leasing business that represented not just Coastal States Producing Company but also Gulf Oil Company, Texas Oil and Gas Company, and other large corporations in the oil industry.

Sanchez and a partner founded the International Bank of Commerce in Laredo in 1966. By 1975, Sanchez had acquired controlling interest in the bank by buying out several investors. At this time his son, Antonio, Jr., joined him in the venture.

In the early 1970s, Sanchez and Brian O'Brien, a geologist from Houston, formed the Sanchez-O'Brien Oil and Gas Corporation. The time was right to start this company, particularly with the 1973 oil crisis in which shipments of foreign oil to the United States were sharply curtailed. Buying up leases for oil and gas exploration was a gamble, but one that Sanchez and O'Brien were willing to take. At one point, nine out of the ten wells they drilled turned out to be producing wells.

As a banker, Sanchez's philosophy is that small businesses applying for bank loans should get the same fair treatment as big businesses in Laredo and nearby border towns. This belief led Sanchez and his son to form, in 1984, what is now a multimillion-dollar banking enterprise known as International Bancshares, a holding company controlling banks. When other banks are not willing to take a gamble on area residents' new business ideas, International Bancshares banks are ready to step in and help. Sanchez started out as a small business owner and understands the needs of small businesses in his community. He has also taken gambles in his career and is not afraid to take a chance on entrepreneurs whose ideas for new businesses are untested.

Sanchez's business associates, as well as his employees, family, and friends, say the key to his success is that he is a hard worker with a positive attitude. He himself has said that perseverance and integrity played a role in his success.

The Sanchez fortunes have continued to grow over the years and now include two additional banks, a construction company, an industrial park, a horse farm, automobile agencies, a Laredo newspaper, and a number of real estate properties. Sanchez-O'Brien Oil and Gas Corporation was ranked number 63 on the *Hispanic Business Magazine* 1990 list of the top 500 Hispanic businesses.

Sources: Matt S. Meier, Mexican American Biographies *(New York: Greenwood Press, 1988), 206; Diana R. Fuentes, "A Texas Dream Becomes a Multimillion Dollar Enterprise,"* Nuestro *8, no. 8 (October 1984); 34–36; and Reed Wolcott, "The Latino Petro-Baron,"* Nuestro *1, no. 4 (July 1977); 21–24.*

ESTIMATING START-UP COSTS

How much money will you need to start your new enterprise? There is no standard answer to this question because each new business is different. For example, money needs vary according to the field of business activity—that is, extractive, manufacturing, wholesaling, retailing, or service. Another determining factor is the size or scale of operations. Obviously your immediate costs will be higher if you have several employees from the start than if yours is a one-person business.

To determine starting costs, you need to estimate your sales volume for the first year. (A method of forecasting sales volume is described in Chapter 4 on pages 88–89.) Since your estimate is likely to differ from the actual sales volume, you should select a conservative estimate. A ***conservative sales estimate*** is one that is more likely to be too low than too high. This is desirable because a high estimate will lead you to invest too much money at the beginning.

You should also select a conservative figure when estimating expenses. A ***conservative expense estimate*** is one that is more likely to be too high than too low. By overestimating expenses, then, you are less likely to get caught short of money.

The two categories of start-up costs are one-time costs and continuing costs. ***One-time costs*** are expenses that will not have to be repeated once the business is under way. The purchase of a sign to be placed on the building is an example. On the other hand, ***continuing costs*** must be paid both at the beginning and throughout the life of the enterprise.

Illustration 7-1
Preparing for a store's grand opening involves costs that will not have to be repeated.

Jeff Greenberg

Examples are rent, telephone, and advertising expenses. Plan to have enough cash on hand to pay continuing costs for more than just the first month. Some experts say you should be prepared for at least the first three months' expenses. Start-up costs are listed in Figure 7-1.

Figure 7-1
Start-up Costs

One-Time Costs

Equipment, machinery, fixtures
Charges for installing equipment, machinery, fixtures
Decorating and remodeling costs
Beginning inventory of merchandise or raw materials
Deposits for utilities
Fees for accountants and lawyers
Licenses and permits
Advertising and sales promotion for "grand opening"
Cash for unexpected needs

Continuing Costs

Salaries for proprietor or partners
Salaries and wages for other employees
Rent
Advertising and sales promotion
Delivery or shipping expenses
Supplies and materials
Utilities (telephone, gas, water, electricity)
Insurance of all types
Taxes (federal, state, local)
Interest on debt
Repairs and maintenance
Fees for accountants and lawyers
Employee training costs
Unexpected needs

Source: Adapted from U.S. Small Business Administration, Checklist for Going into Business, *Management Aids no. 2.016 (Washington, DC: U.S. Government Printing Office, 1982), 4.*

TYPES OF FUNDS

The two types of funds for businesses are equity funds and debt funds. In operating their businesses, most entrepreneurs use a combination of these two types.

EQUITY FUNDS

Equity is another word for ownership. Thus, ***equity funds*** consist of money or capital contributed by owners. Entrepreneurs' personal sources of money include savings, retirement benefits, sale of a home, or inheritance. If sufficient start-up money cannot be obtained from personal sources of equity, an entrepreneur may take in a partner or form a corporation and sell shares of stock. Since, in many cases, there is not enough equity money available, entrepreneurs resort to debt funds.

DEBT FUNDS

Debt funds are dollars or capital you borrow. Banks, other financial institutions, and individuals are all sources of debt funds. The privilege of paying for goods and services after they have been delivered or provided is ***credit.*** Suppliers of merchandise or equipment may sell to businesses on credit terms. When entrepreneurs borrow money or use credit, a charge is involved known as ***interest.***

COMPARISON OF FUNDS

An entrepreneur should use both equity funds and debt funds for sources of capital. The type of funds used depends on these factors: risk, control, and availability.

RISK. There is little risk to the enterprise with equity capital. Owners do not have to be repaid. By contrast, great risk is involved with debt funds. Failure to make loan payments when they are due could cause lenders to require that the loan be repaid in full immediately. An entrepreneur may have to sell real estate or other business property to obtain sufficient money to repay a loan, or lenders may take ownership of the entire business.

CONTROL. An owner's degree of control is usually directly related to the percentage of ownership. That is, the more ownership an entrepreneur has, the more authority the entrepreneur will have regarding the operation of the business. Entrepreneurs lose some control of their businesses every time they take in a partner or sell shares of stock. An entrepreneur who started a business to be a boss may suddenly feel as though others are in control. On the other hand, lenders do not ordinarily get actively involved in the operation of their borrowers' businesses.

AVAILABILITY. At a particular time, either debt funds or equity funds could be difficult to obtain. Debt funds may not be available to the business because of high interest rates, the entrepreneur's poor personal credit record, or a history of low earnings or losses for the enterprise. The only sources of available funds may be to obtain equity from new partners or to sell stock. In other situations, an entrepreneur may be unable to find equity investors, leaving the entrepreneur with no alternative but to borrow the money.

SOURCES OF FUNDS

Equity funds are invested in the business by an entrepreneur, one or more partners, or stockholders. These people are owners and are usually willing to wait months or years to be repaid. Therefore, equity funds are usually considered to be long-term funds. In contrast, some debt funds are short-term and must be repaid quickly, while others are long-term.

Businesses need both current assets and fixed assets. ***Current assets*** are cash and any other assets that can be easily and quickly turned into cash. Inventory and accounts receivable are examples of current assets. ***Inventory*** may include raw materials, finished goods, or supplies. ***Accounts receivable*** are sums of money owed to the business by customers.

Fixed assets are items that the business expects to own for more than one year. These items are not used up, or converted into cash, in a short period of time. Typical examples are land, buildings, equipment, and trucks.

The key to successful business financing is to obtain current assets with short-term loans or credit and to obtain fixed assets with long-term loans. For example, an entrepreneur should consider a 90-day bank loan to buy inventory or a 15-year loan to buy property.

SHORT-TERM LOANS OR CREDIT

Short-term loans and credit are available from vendors, commercial banks, commercial finance companies, and factors.

VENDORS. Vendors are businesses from which entrepreneurs buy products. While vendors do not usually lend money, they will often supply merchandise and allow businesses to pay for the merchandise by a specified date. Under this arrangement, known as ***trade credit,*** entrepreneurs may have 30 or more days to pay their bills. The exact credit terms depend on the line of trade and the credit rating of the enterprise. To those who have satisfactory payment records, a vendor may extend credit interest-free. An advantage of trade credit is that an entrepreneur may sell the merchandise to obtain the money needed to pay a vendor's bill.

COMMERCIAL BANKS. Local commercial banks are one of the best sources of short-term loans. The primary short-term loan is the ***commercial loan,*** usually made for 90 to 180 days. This loan is generally made without any specific ***collateral,*** which is something of value the borrower pledges to the bank as security for the loan. Commercial loans are advanced to profitable businesses with good credit ratings. Entrepreneurs are required to repay commercial loans in a lump sum.

When many of the current assets are held in unpaid customer accounts and the enterprise needs more cash, an accounts receivable loan may be the answer. Available from commercial banks, ***accounts receivable loans*** involve the pledging of accounts receivable as collateral for a short-term loan. This type of loan allows an entrepreneur to convert unpaid customer accounts into cash. Banks usually advance up to 80 percent of the value of the accounts receivable, allowing themselves some protection for uncollectible accounts. Typically, the accounts receivable loan is set up as a revolving line of credit for the business borrower. In a ***revolving line of credit,*** funds are continually advanced to the enterprise, repaid, and advanced once again. The entrepreneur pays interest on the remaining balance of the loan.

Commercial banks also engage in inventory financing. With ***inventory financing,*** an entrepreneur pledges inventory as collateral for short-term funds to receive a revolving line of credit. Entrepreneurs repay inventory loans as cash flows into the enterprise from the sale of items in inventory.

When an established business is profitable, the enterprise may qualify for an unsecured line of credit. For this type of loan, no collateral is pledged. Generally, an entrepreneur may borrow, repay, and borrow again within a one-year period.

COMMERCIAL FINANCE COMPANIES. ***Commercial finance companies*** are specialists in accounts receivable and inventory loans. They often combine the collateral of accounts receivable and inventory loans to provide a business with a larger line of credit. They seldom make unsecured loans to small businesses.

Illustration 7-2
A commercial bank (left) and a commercial finance company offer different kinds of services to borrowers.

FACTORS. Entrepreneurs may pledge accounts receivable as collateral for a loan, and they can also sell accounts receivable to obtain short-term funds for the business. Selling accounts receivable is called ***factoring.*** Financial firms that buy accounts receivable are ***factors.*** Factors purchase the accounts receivable at less than face value and then collect the full amounts from customers when payments are due. While this service has a cost, businesses obtain funds without waiting for customers to pay their bills.

LONG-TERM LOANS

In most cases, part of the financing of the new enterprise will consist of long-term loans, also known as ***term loans.*** Term loans are extended for more than one year and are used to obtain land, buildings, equipment, and other fixed assets. Some commercial banks and commercial finance companies make both short-term loans and long-term loans. Equipment manufacturers and distributors also provide long-term financing.

COMMERCIAL BANKS. One of the primary sources of long-term loans, particularly those extended for three to five years, is the commercial bank. The bank's installment loan department generally processes long-term loans. Most commercial banks require a written loan agreement for a long-term loan. The agreement may limit the amount of salary entrepreneurs pay themselves or require them to obtain approval from the bank before borrowing money from other sources. The bank may also require a compensating balance. A ***compensating balance*** is a sum of money deposited in the bank for the duration of the loan to serve as collateral. Commercial banks may offer term loans with personal guarantees, equipment loans, and real estate loans.

Term Loans with Personal Guarantees. Through ***personal guarantees,*** borrowers agree to pay the unpaid balance of the loan if the business, including a corporation, is unable to repay it. Asking for a personal guarantee is standard procedure for small business loans, especially when the business is not yet operating. This permits the bank to recover its money if the business fails. The personal guarantee is also a measure of the entrepreneur's confidence in the business.

Equipment Loans. ***Equipment loans*** enable an enterprise to buy new equipment or to obtain funds when the firm does not qualify for unsecured credit. Most banks limit their equipment loans to between 60 and 80 percent of the value of the equipment. The loans are usually repaid in monthly installments for a maximum of five years, depending on the useful life of the equipment.

Real Estate Loans. ***Real estate loans*** are usually made for up to 75 percent of the value of the land and/or buildings and repaid over 10 to 20 years. The bank will require a ***first mortgage*** as security for the real estate loan. If the borrower fails to make the payments, ownership of the property will be transferred to the bank.

COMMERCIAL FINANCE COMPANIES. The three types of long-term financing offered by commercial finance companies are equipment loans, real estate loans, and equipment leasing. Equipment loans are provided in the same form as those granted by commercial banks. The loan period is determined by the useful life of the equipment. The equipment serves as collateral for the loan, and funds are advanced to cover up to 80 percent of the cost of the equipment.

Likewise, commercial finance companies offer real estate loans similar to those offered by the commercial banks. However, these loans are not available from all commercial finance companies.

Through ***equipment leasing,*** individuals may obtain and use equipment without owning it. Rather than paying for equipment in one lump sum, lease payments are made as the equipment is used. Cash that would otherwise be tied up in a fixed asset is available to buy inventory or pay current expenses.

EQUIPMENT MANUFACTURERS AND DISTRIBUTORS. To encourage entrepreneurs to buy their equipment, manufacturers and distributors often will finance the purchase. This can be an important source of funds but only for the amount of the purchase price. Usually a down payment is required, and the balance is paid in monthly installments. The payment period may extend over one or more years, depending on the type and price of the equipment.

NEEDS FOR ADDITIONAL CAPITAL

As a business grows, so does the need for more and more capital. Some of the more common factors creating this need are sales growth, expansion of the business, opportunities to reduce costs, seasonal factors, and economic conditions.

SALES GROWTH

To keep up with an increasing sales volume, an entrepreneur will have to continually buy more inventory. Because the goods must be available and ready for sale when customers want them, an entrepreneur must buy inventory at a rate faster than the increase in sales.

Sales growth can create a larger volume of accounts receivable. In addition, sales growth requires the business to have larger amounts of cash to pay wages to more employees and to pay increased expenses brought about by increased sales. The business must sometimes borrow money until customers pay their bills.

EXPANSION

When entrepreneurs expand to open an office at an additional location or to include a new product or service line, they need more capital. Sometimes these expenses equal or exceed the initial start-up costs of establishing the business.

OPPORTUNITIES TO REDUCE COSTS

Sometimes entrepreneurs must be prepared to spend money to save money in the long run. For example, an entrepreneur may have the opportunity to buy new machinery that will lower the cost of producing the firm's primary product. Another example is spending money for more efficient heating and cooling equipment to reduce the firm's utility bill.

An entrepreneur may receive substantial savings by taking advantage of quantity discounts on inventory purchases. A ***quantity discount*** is a reduction in price as a result of the amount purchased. The discount could be based on the amount of one particular item ordered or on the total amount of all items. For example, an order for 500 items at $10 each instead of a usual order of 100 items may qualify the buyer for a 5 percent discount. The discount saves the buyer 50 cents per item. However, the entrepreneur must have cash or be able to arrange credit to take advantage of the discount offer.

SEASONAL FACTORS

Rather than having a constant level of sales from month to month, many businesses experience peaks and valleys in their sales volumes. For example, toy manufacturers sell a large part of their annual production in a few months each year. Retailers and wholesalers order toys in the spring and summer months for delivery prior to the Christmas gift buying season. Likewise, suppliers of school furniture sell a major portion of their products for delivery just prior to the beginning of the school year. As a result, large amounts of cash flow into these businesses in some months, while little or no cash flows in during other months. Seasonal needs can create a need for additional capital. To prepare for major selling seasons, entrepreneurs may have to borrow money to buy additional materials and supplies and to hire more employees.

ECONOMIC CONDITIONS

Local or national economic conditions may cause temporary decreases in sales and profits. For example, other businesses in the community suffer when manufacturing plants close, leaving employees without jobs. The jobless people do not have the spending ability they once had, thereby reducing the sales of other businesses in the community. Business owners may need to borrow money to pay expenses until conditions improve. Rent, utilities, and wages must be paid, even when the sales volume is low.

TIPS FOR REQUESTING LOANS

Entrepreneurs should prepare themselves for meeting with a lender to apply for a loan. While this discussion deals with commercial banks, many of the suggestions also pertain to obtaining loans from other types of lenders.

Tips that may improve the entrepreneur's chances of obtaining a bank loan are (1) selecting the bank carefully, (2) preparing financial statements, (3) making an appointment, (4) preparing to answer typical questions, and (5) preparing to guarantee the loan.

SELECT THE BANK CAREFULLY

Some banks deal mostly with large corporations. Others aim to serve consumers and perhaps small businesses. Entrepreneurs should select banks that specialize in making loans to businesses, particularly those banks having a history of working with firms similar in size and type to theirs. Loan processing time may be reduced when the banker is familiar with the industry, the products and services sold, and the customers.

If, for reasons beyond their control, entrepreneurs are unable to make loan payments on time, a banker who understands the business may be willing to make other arrangements for repayment. Other lenders may not be as willing to discuss alternatives for repaying the loan.

PREPARE FINANCIAL STATEMENTS

The lending officer of the bank will ask to see a complete set of financial statements. Although some entrepreneurs prepare these statements themselves, it is wiser to have an accountant prepare the financial statements to be assured of a thorough financial file. Without assistance from an accountant, an entrepreneur may not borrow enough money in the beginning. Having to return for additional loans later could make the lending officer suspect that the entrepreneur does not know how to operate the business and may be a poor risk.

MAKE AN APPOINTMENT

People walk into banks and apply for credit cards and car loans every day. This is the common practice for these transactions. When seeking a business loan, however, it is customary to make an appointment. Entrepreneurs who ask for appointments show they are business-minded.

Illustration 7-3
Meeting with a business officer to obtain a business loan takes careful preparation.

PREPARE TO ANSWER TYPICAL QUESTIONS

The lending officers of commercial banks will ask questions to determine whether the borrower qualifies for a loan. Entrepreneurs should be prepared to answer these typical questions:

- *How do you plan to spend the money?* The funds should be used for equipment, inventory, or other expenses directly related to the sales and profits of the business. A loan request is generally approved only if the money will be used directly in the business or if the plan is to start a low-risk venture.

- *How much money do you need?* Entrepreneurs should request neither too much nor too little money. The more specific borrowers are in answering this question, the more likely they are to get the loan.
- *When do you need the money?* A committee will review loan requests. Because committee reviews of loan applications take time, borrowers should apply early for a bank loan before their funds are gone. Lenders look more favorably on those who plan ahead.
- *When will the loan be repaid?* The shorter the period of time the money is needed, the better the chances of getting the loan. Bankers associate shorter time periods with lower risk.
- *What is the source of the money for repaying the loan?* Bankers will need to know how an entrepreneur plans to repay the loan. Money borrowed to buy inventory, for example, can be repaid when the inventory is sold.

PREPARE TO GUARANTEE THE LOAN

Even the best credit prospects should be prepared to personally guarantee their loans. If the business fails, the entrepreneurs may have to sell personal and family property to repay a business loan. Clearly, this involves risk. On the other hand, if entrepreneurs are not willing to risk their assets, why should banks risk theirs?

ACTION STEPS FOR ASPIRING ENTREPRENEURS

Use these action steps to help you prepare for the possibility of being an entrepreneur at some point in your career:

1. Ask entrepreneurs for tips on estimating sales and expenses.
2. Think about how you would feel owning a business with a partner. You would give up some control by having a partner; however, the partner may be able to invest the funds that are needed in the business.
3. Learn as much as you can about different types of loans and credit.
4. Develop money management skills that will help you to be economical now in your personal spending and, later, in your business.

BUILDING YOUR ENTERPRISE VOCABULARY

Match the following terms with the statements that best describe applications of those terms. Write the letter of your choice in the space provided.

a. one-time costs
b. equity
c. current assets
d. fixed assets
e. trade credit
f. collateral
g. factors
h. equipment leasing
i. personal guarantees
j. quantity discount

_______ 1. Cash is an example.
_______ 2. Security for a loan.
_______ 3. Incurred when setting up the business.
_______ 4. "Save 3% on orders of more than 100 units."
_______ 5. You may be able to sell the merchandise before you have paid for it.
_______ 6. You are the owner.
_______ 7. Firms that buy accounts receivable.
_______ 8. Agreeing to repay a loan made to the business.
_______ 9. Buildings and trucks are examples.
_______ 10. Being able to use equipment without owning it.

UNDERSTANDING KEY CONCEPTS

Write a short answer to each of the following questions.

1. Why should conservative sales estimates and conservative expense estimates be used?

____

____

____

____

2. Explain the difference between one-time costs and continuing costs. Give an example of each.

____

____

____

____

____

3. What is the difference between equity funds and debt funds?

4. What factors should the entrepreneur consider when deciding whether to use debt funds or equity funds in a particular situation? Explain each of these factors.

5. What types of assets should be obtained with short-term loans or credit? Which assets should be obtained with long-term loans?

6. List four sources of short-term loans or credit.

7. List three sources of long-term loans.

____

____

____

8. Give five reasons why businesses may need more and more capital as they grow.

____

____

____

____

____

APPLYING YOUR ENTERPRISE KNOWLEDGE

These activities will give you a chance to apply what you have learned in Chapter 7.

1. List the names, addresses, and telephone numbers of up to three commercial banks in your community.

   Name of bank: ____

   Address: ____

   Telephone number: ____

   Name of bank: ____

   Address: ____

   Telephone number: ____

   Name of bank: ____

   Address: ____

   Telephone number: ____

2. Make an appointment to interview an entrepreneur who is familiar with the type of business you plan to start. For each of the sources of funds listed below, ask the entrepreneur what assets each source would be used to finance. Record your answers in the appropriate spaces below.

Sources of Funds	Assets Financed by the Source
Vendors	
Commercial banks	
Commercial finance companies	
Factors	
Equipment manufacturers and distributors	

SOLVING BUSINESS PROBLEMS: ARNOLD CONSTRUCTION COMPANY

In six months or less, Anita and Roger Arnold plan to have their construction company in operation. They have twelve years of construction experience between them, and they believe they know what it takes to run a successful company.

Roger prepared a list of rough estimates of all the one-time costs and continuing costs for the new enterprise. Anita, an experienced accountant, closely reviewed each item on the list and revised the figures where necessary. Finally, Anita and Roger reviewed the list together until they were confident that each cost estimate was as accurate as possible. Now that the Arnolds know what their costs will be, they are not certain how or where they will obtain the funds to start the business.

Ethan Gates, a former construction company owner, contacted Anita and Roger. He offered to invest in their business and become their partner. Gates's investment would be larger than Anita and Roger's investment. The Arnolds are flattered that someone would come to them and offer to buy into their business. They also like the idea that, with Mr. Gates's investment, they would not have to borrow any money. At the same time, they do not want to accept anyone's investment until they have had a chance to think about all the alternatives available to them. They are also wondering why Mr. Gates is interested in their business when it is not yet in operation.

Before the Arnolds accept Mr. Gates's offer, they are considering visiting a bank to discuss the possibility of obtaining a loan.

1. Would you advise the Arnolds to use only equity funds in starting their business? Why or why not?

2. Why do you believe Ethan Gates wants to invest in Arnold Construction Company?

3. What should the Arnolds do to prepare to meet with the loan officer at the commercial bank?

BUSINESS PLAN PROJECT

Use the space provided on pages 183 and 184 for the business plan activities below.

1. List the start-up costs for your enterprise, including both the one-time costs and the continuing costs.

2. Estimate the amount of equity funds and/or debt funds that you will use to start the business.

SAMPLE

START-UP COSTS

One-Time Costs

Equipment, machinery, fixtures	$ ______________	
Charges for installation	______________	
Decorating and remodeling	______________	
Beginning inventory	______________	
Deposits for utilities	______________	
Fees for accountants and lawyers	______________	
Licenses and permits	______________	
Promotion methods at "grand opening"	______________	
Cash for unexpected needs	______________	
TOTAL ONE-TIME COSTS		$ ______________

Continuing Costs for Three Months

All wages and salaries	$ ______________	
Rent	______________	
Advertising and sales promotion	______________	
Delivery expenses	______________	
Supplies and materials	______________	
Utilities	______________	
Insurance of all types	______________	
Taxes (federal, state, local)	______________	
Interest on debt	______________	
Repairs and maintenance	______________	
Fees for accountants and lawyers	______________	
Employee training costs	______________	
Unexpected needs	______________	
TOTAL CONTINUING COSTS FOR THREE MONTHS		$ ______________
TOTAL START-UP COSTS		$ ______________

Source: Adapted from U.S. Small Business Administration, Checklist for Going into Business, *Management Aids no. 2.016 (Washington, DC: U.S. Government Printing Office, 1982), 4.*

SOURCES OF FUNDS

Sources of Equity Funds	Amount	
Personal savings	$ ________	
Partners	________	
Sale of stock in a corporation	________	
TOTAL EQUITY FUNDS		$ ________

Sources of Debt Funds		
____________________	$ ________	
____________________	________	
____________________	________	
TOTAL DEBT FUNDS		$ ________
TOTAL OF EQUITY FUNDS AND DEBT FUNDS*		$ ________

*The total of equity funds and debt funds should equal total start-up costs.

CHAPTER 8

PREPARING THE FINANCIAL PLAN

Some entrepreneurs run into financial difficulty even when they attain high sales volumes. Their concern with the day-to-day operation of their enterprises causes them to overlook the part of the business plan that will tell them if, and when, they will make a profit. They have neglected financial planning. You will learn about this critical part of the business plan in this chapter. Through ***financial planning,*** you will describe your business plan in terms of dollars.

Learning Objectives

After you have studied Chapter 8, you should be able to:

1. Prepare a cash budget, an income statement, and a balance sheet.
2. Describe how price, volume, cost of sales, and operating expenses affect net profit.

ENTREPRENEUR PROFILE Lillian Vernon

Lillian Vernon is the chief executive officer of the mail-order business she started in 1951 when she was 24 years old. The company, a leader in the catalog industry, specializes in gifts, decorative and home accessories, housewares, and toys. With a customer mailing list of 12.5 million people, the firm generates annual sales of over $162 million.

Lillian Vernon was born in 1927 in Leipzig, Germany, to parents known as hard-working and scrupulously honest. The family moved to Holland in 1933. Then, in 1937, when war in Europe was likely, the family emigrated to the United States and selected New York City as its new home. Her father started a small leather goods manufacturing company.

Lillian worked after school as an usher in a movie theater and as a sales clerk in a candy store. Even though she hated numbers, she was elected treasurer of her high school class. After completing her high school education, Lillian went on to New York University where she majored in psychology, but dropped out after two years to start her business.

At age 24, and pregnant with her first child, Lillian was looking for a way to make some money to supplement the $75 weekly salary of her husband. Because she would be staying home with her child, Lillian needed a home-based business rather than a full-time job outside the home. She started a mail-order business on her kitchen table. The "venture capital" consisted of $2,000 of money received as wedding gifts. This was the only money she had, and she put it all into the business. Originally known as Vernon Specialties Company, the firm's name was later changed to Lillian Vernon Corporation.

Lillian's goal was to offer by mail products that could not be easily found in retail stores or were not available at reasonable prices. Her first two products were a leather handbag and a belt that she personalized. It did not take Lillian long to find out that the buying public was as excited about her products as she was. A mail-order advertisement she purchased for $495 in the September 1951 issue of *Seventeen* magazine generated $32,000 in sales in six weeks. This return on a single advertisement was remarkable, particularly when you consider that the company name was not familiar to prospective customers. Revenues generated by this first advertisement were poured back into the company and used to buy more handbags, belts, and advertisements.

Even as Lillian's company was growing, she continued managing it around her two young children's schedules. She did the shopping for the family and took her turns driving in car pools for school activities. She began to devote full time to the company when both sons went to college. Annual sales grew from $1 million in 1970 to $137 million in 1986, which marked Lillian's thirty-fifth year in business. By 1992, company sales volume exceeded $162 million and a profit of $9 million.

When starting your own business, Lillian suggests that you pay as you go and live on a budget. She also knows that success does not come easily and that there are four ingredients of success: objectivity, a desire for achievement, dedication, and developing and trusting your instincts.

Lillian Vernon has faced many challenges in good times and bad. In 1984, for example, too-rapid growth coupled with a new computer system that failed to live up to expectations caused the company to become overstocked. The company was in trouble. Lillian reacted by cutting expenses, reducing the number of employees, and liquidating excess inventory. In 1987, the company's stock was sold to the public for the first time. Lillian was faced with a new challenge, that of having to consider the stockholders' interests in every major business decision. After the October 1987 stock market crash, the corporation's stock lost more than half its value.

Under Lillian's leadership, the company continues to grow at a rate of 10 percent per year. She spends sixteen weeks each year traveling throughout the world selecting products to be featured in her catalogs. Lillian's two sons, who grew up watching their mother run the business, are now involved in the senior management of the company.

Sources: Robert D. Hisrich and Michael P. Peters, Entrepreneurship: Starting, Developing, and Managing a New Enterprise, *2d ed. (Homewood, IL: Richard D. Irwin, 1992), 49–51, and Russel R. Taylor,* Exceptional Entrepreneurial Women: Strategies for Success *(New York: Quorum Books, 1988), 21–24.*

FINANCIAL STATEMENTS

Financial statements can take various forms depending on how they are to be used. Their purpose is to document important facts about an enterprise's operation. The business plan for a new enterprise should include three financial statements: a cash budget, an income statement, and a balance sheet.

CASH BUDGET

A ***cash budget*** is a measure of changes in the cash an enterprise will have available from month to month. Businesses use cash budgets to estimate cash needs for a period in the future, usually twelve months.

The first step in preparing a cash budget is to determine the ***cash balance*** at the beginning of the month. This shows how much cash is on hand (e.g., in cash registers) and in the bank.

The second step is to estimate cash receipts. ***Cash receipts*** include all funds that will be received from cash sales, collection of credit sales, and loans. This estimate will be based on your sales forecast. When cash receipts are added to cash balance, the sum is the total cash available for use by the business during the month.

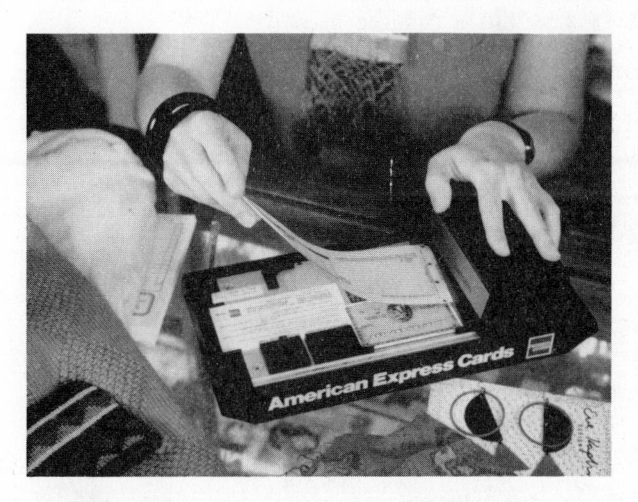

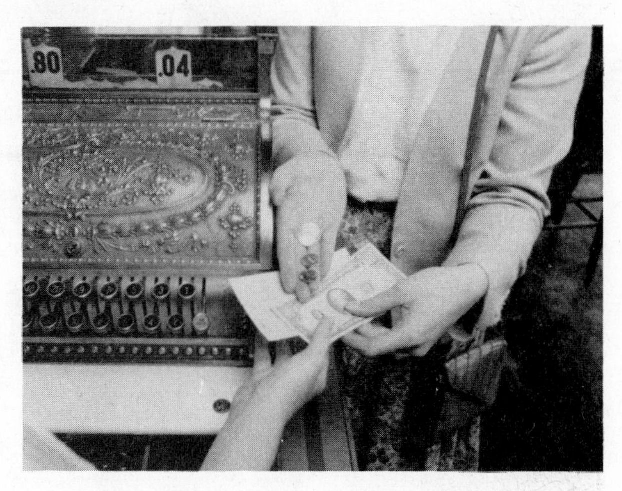

Illustration 8-1
Cash receipts include funds received from collection of credit sales (left) and cash sales.

The next step in the budget process is to estimate ***cash disbursements.*** These refer to cash that will have to be paid out during the month for purchases and for operating or continuing expenses. The largest cash outlays are usually for merchandise and wages and salaries.

Finally, when you subtract total cash disbursements from total cash available, the result is the cash balance at the end of the month. This figure then becomes the beginning cash balance for the next month.

The cash budget formula is:

Beginning Cash Balance for MONTH 1
+ Cash Receipts
= Total Cash Available
– Total Cash Disbursements
= Cash Balance at End of MONTH 1
= Beginning Cash Balance for MONTH 2

To further explain how a cash budget is prepared, let us assume that Chris and Manuel are planning to open a T-shirt shop on July 1. All the one-time costs of start-up have been paid and they have $2,000 in cash.

Chris and Manuel have decided to sell only on a cash basis, at least for the time being. They estimate their sales for the first three months as follows: $3,000 in July, $4,000 in August, and $4,800 in September. They believe their cash disbursements for those months will be $3,200, $4,100, and $4,900 respectively.

As their cash budget shows (see Figure 8-1), sales increase each month, but the cash balance decreases because their expenses increase each month. This may be a signal that the business is heading for trouble. Without the cash budget, the partners might not have learned of the problem until it was too late. At least now they have time to do something about it. For example, they should find out if they are overspending in some areas. Maybe they have spent too much on merchandise, or they may want to arrange for a loan in case the cash balance continues to slide. The loan could then be repaid when the cash situation improves.

Figure 8-1
Cash Budget

Chris & Manuel's T-Shirt Shop
Cash Budget
For Quarter Ending September 30, 19--

	July	August	September
Beginning Cash Balance	$2,000.00	$1,800.00	$1,700.00
Cash Receipts:			
Cash Sales	3,000.00	4,000.00	4,800.00
Credit Sales Payments	-0-	-0-	-0-
Loans	-0-	-0-	-0-
Total Cash Available	$5,000.00	$5,800.00	$6,500.00
Total Cash Disbursements for Month	3,200.00	4,100.00	4,900.00
Cash Balance at End of Month	$1,800.00	$1,700.00	$1,600.00

INCOME STATEMENT

The ***income statement*** shows how a business has performed over a certain period of time. It is also referred to as a ***profit-and-loss statement.***

Some entrepreneurs prepare income statements just once a year; others do so more frequently. An entrepreneur of a new enterprise should prepare an income statement every month, or at least every three months. You will then have a better idea of how the business is operating. If problems occur, you will be able to take quick action.

The parts included in an income statement are sales, cost of sales, gross profit, expenses, and net profit. An example of an income statement is given in Figure 8-2.

Figure 8-2
Income Statement

Early American Home Furnishings Income Statement For Year Ended December 31, 19--		
Sales		$89,550.00
Cost of Sales		43,879.00
Gross Profit		45,671.00
Expenses:		
Wages and Salaries	$13,351.00	
Rent	7,800.00	
Advertising and Sales Promotion	1,305.00	
Delivery Expenses	896.00	
Supplies and Materials	1,195.00	
Utilities	1,791.00	
Insurance	725.00	
Taxes (but not federal income tax)	1,164.00	
Interest on Debt	448.00	
Repairs and Maintenance	695.00	
Fees for Accountants and Lawyers	1,050.00	
Employee Training Costs	240.00	
Other Expenses	1,075.00	
Total Expenses		31,735.00
Net Profit (before income tax)		$13,936.00

The term ***sales*** refers to all income that flows into the business from sales activity. Extractive enterprises, manufacturers, wholesalers, and retailers obtain this income from the sale of goods. Service businesses derive their sales income from fees charged when services are provided.

Cost of sales represents the cost of the products or services sold in a given time period. Cost of sales is called ***cost of goods sold*** by retailers and wholesalers. It represents what they pay for products they sell. In manufacturing, cost of sales is known as ***cost of goods manufactured.*** It includes only those costs directly associated with making the product. A service business may calculate the ***cost of services*** sold based on wages paid to persons providing the service.

Gross profit, known as ***gross margin*** when stated as a percentage, is determined by subtracting cost of sales from sales. Gross profit should not be confused with net profit, a term to be described below. The formula for calculating gross profit is:

$$\text{Gross Profit} = \text{Sales} - \text{Cost of Sales}$$

Expenses are all the costs of running an enterprise other than those included in the cost of sales. Many continuing costs are expenses. Some of the items included are advertising, insurance, rent, utilities, and interest on debt.

Net profit is the income remaining after paying all expenses, including taxes.

The parts of an income statement are related as follows:

$$\text{Net Profit} = \text{Sales} - \text{Cost of Sales} - \text{Expenses}$$

or

$$\text{Net Profit} = \text{Gross Profit} - \text{Expenses}$$

Illustration 8-2
Keeping lights on after-hours is one of the expenses of running a store.

A ***projected income statement*** is based on the entrepreneur's estimates of sales, cost of sales, and expenses for the first year. Such a statement should be included in every business plan. Without a projected income statement, the entrepreneur will not be able to determine the profit potential of the new enterprise.

When the business is actually in operation, data will be available to prepare a regular income statement. That is, the statement would be based on actual rather than projected figures.

BALANCE SHEET

The ***balance sheet*** is used to keep track of what an enterprise owns, what it owes, and what the owner has invested (see Figure 8-3). A balance sheet is like a picture of the enterprise's assets and the claims against those assets for a particular date.

This financial statement is called a balance sheet because assets balance with, or are equal to, liabilities plus net worth. This is shown as follows:

Assets = Liabilities + Net Worth

Assets are items or possessions used in the business which have monetary value. On the balance sheet, assets are divided into three groups: current assets, fixed assets, and intangible assets.

Current assets are those which the enterprise would not expect to hold longer than one year. This group includes cash as well as other items that can be easily and quickly converted to cash. Examples are merchandise in inventory and ***accounts receivable,*** which are sums of money owed to the enterprise by customers.

Figure 8-3
Balance Sheet

Mike's Auto Parts
Balance Sheet
December 31, 19--

ASSETS		
Current Assets:		
Cash	$ 2,815.00	
Inventory	27,950.00	
Accounts Receivable	1,250.00	
Total Current Assets		$ 32,015.00
Fixed Assets:		
Land	$12,000.00	
Building	49,500.00	
Equipment	10,500.00	
Total Fixed Assets		$ 72,000.00
Intangible Assets:		
Goodwill	$ 1,500.00	
Other Intangible Assets	-0-	
Total Intangible Assets		$ 1,500.00
Total Assets		$105,515.00
LIABILITIES		
Current Liabilities:		
Accounts Payable	$ 6,505.00	
Notes Payable	1,345.00	
Accrued Expenses	825.00	
Total Current Liabilities		$ 8,675.00
Fixed Liabilities:		
Long-Term Loan	$ 9,275.00	
Mortgage	55,210.00	
Total Fixed Liabilities		$ 64,485.00
Total Liabilities		$ 73,160.00
NET WORTH		
Owner's Capital		$ 32,355.00
Total Liabilities and Net Worth		$105,515.00

Fixed assets are items that the business expects to own for more than one year. These items are not used up, or converted into cash, in a short period of time. Typical examples are land, buildings, equipment, and trucks.

The third group of assets is ***intangible assets.*** These assets have value and are useful to the enterprise, but they do not exist in a physical sense. A common example is goodwill, which you may have to pay for when buying an existing enterprise. ***Goodwill*** is the extra money paid because the enterprise has a good reputation. Other intangible assets found in balance sheets are copyrights, patents, and franchises.

Liabilities are debts of the enterprise. They are usually divided into two groups: current liabilities and fixed liabilities.

Current liabilities are debts that are due to be paid in one year or less. Debts commonly included in this category are:

Accounts payable —Amounts owed to suppliers for goods and services provided.

Notes payable —Short-term loans that have to be repaid within a year.

Accrued expenses —Expenses incurred but not yet paid, such as wages that have been earned but not yet paid.

Debts that are due to be paid in more than a year are called ***fixed liabilities.*** They are also known as ***long-term liabilities.*** Mortgages and long-term loans are examples.

The excess of the value of the assets over the value of the liabilities is called ***net worth.*** This includes all money invested by owners, known as ***owner's capital,*** plus accumulated profits, less withdrawals. The method for computing net worth is:

Net Worth = Total Assets – Total Liabilities

The balance sheet is important because it reveals the enterprise's ability to repay both long-term and short-term debts. For this reason, bankers and other lenders often ask to see this financial statement before lending money.

BASIC PROFIT VARIABLES

Entrepreneurs make countless decisions about how their businesses are to operate. Some decisions are made infrequently and have long-term effects. An example is the decision to select a location for the enterprise. Other decisions, such as setting the price for an item, are made more frequently and have short-term effects. Ultimately, however, all decisions are related to the four basic profit variables of price, volume of sales, cost of sales, and operating expenses. A change in any one of the variables affects net profit.

As shown in Figure 8-4, the owners of Fiesta Bicycle Shop estimate that they will sell 1,000 bicycles at a price of $100 each. Total sales for the year will be $100,000. The owners also expect to pay $60 for each bicycle and to incur $35,000 in operating expenses during the year.

Figure 8-4
Fiesta Bicycle Shop Projected Income Statement

Fiesta Bicycle Shop
Projected Income Statement
For Year Ended December 31, 19--

	Original Estimate
Sales (1,000 units @ $100)	$100,000
Cost of Sales (1,000 units @ $60)	60,000
Gross Profit	40,000
Operating Expenses	35,000
Net Profit	$ 5,000

Assume that Fiesta's owners want to see how changes in the basic profit variables would affect the original estimates shown in Figure 8-4. The series of income statements in Figures 8-5 through 8-8 (pages 193–196) will illustrate the impact of these changes.

A CHANGE IN PRICE

One way to increase profits is to raise prices. Assume that the owners of Fiesta Bicycle Shop could raise prices by 5 percent, or $5, and still sell 1,000 bicycles during the year. Perhaps they are able to do this because their prices are not as high as their competitors' prices. With the price increase of 5 percent, the selling price for each bicycle would be $105. The sales figure on the income statement would be determined as follows: 1,000 bicycles × $105 = $105,000. The effect on net profit is shown in Figure 8-5.

Figure 8-5
Projected Income Statement with Change in Price

Fiesta Bicycle Shop
Projected Income Statement
For Year Ended December 31, 19--

	Change in Price	Original Estimate
Sales (1,000 units @ $105)	$105,000	$100,000
Cost of Sales (1,000 units @ $60)	60,000	60,000
Gross Profit	45,000	40,000
Operating Expenses	35,000	35,000
Net Profit	$ 10,000	$ 5,000

The percent by which a number increases or decreases can be determined by following two steps. First, find the dollar amount of the increase or decrease from the original estimate. Second, divide the dollar amount of the increase or decrease by the original estimate. The answer is the percent by which the number increased or decreased.

Notice that if the owners raised prices by 5 percent, net profit would increase by 100 percent, from $5,000 to $10,000. This example points out the importance of making sound pricing decisions. Even small increases in prices can improve profits. Charging prices that are too low can lower profits or cause losses.

A CHANGE IN VOLUME OF SALES

Prices charged for individual products and the number of units sold, or ***volume***, together determine the sales figure appearing on the income statement. Rather than increasing their prices, assume now that the owners of Fiesta Bicycle Shop want to see what would happen if they lower their prices. Specifically, they believe that they could sell 1,200 bicycles, instead of 1,000, if they lower the price by 5 percent, or $5. The selling price becomes $95. On the income statement, the sales figure would be the product of multiplying $95 by 1,200, or $114,000. The effect on net profit of this change in sales volume is shown in Figure 8-6.

Figure 8-6
Projected Income Statement with Change in Volume

Fiesta Bicycle Shop
Projected Income Statement
For Year Ended December 31, 19--

	Change in Volume	Original Estimate
Sales (1,200 units @ $95)	$114,000	$100,000
Cost of Sales (1,200 units @ $60)	72,000	60,000
Gross Profit	42,000	40,000
Operating Expenses	35,000	35,000
Net Profit	$ 7,000	$ 5,000

Net profit will increase from $5,000 to $7,000 if the shop can sell 200 more bicycles at the lower price of $95. Note that the increase in sales volume was accompanied by an increase in cost of sales. This, of course, is a result of the need to buy 200 additional bicycles for resale. In this example, the selling price was reduced by 5 percent, while sales volume increased by 20 percent and profit increased by 40 percent.

Illustration 8-3
Having a sale is a way to increase volume and net profit.

A CHANGE IN COST OF SALES

Another way to increase net profit is to reduce cost of sales. Assume that Fiesta Bicycle Shop's owners have decided to replace the bicycle line they now carry with another manufacturer's bicycle. The new product is equal in quality to the current product, but it costs 5 percent less, or $57 per bicycle. In Figure 8-7, sales are $100,000 and the cost of sales is $57,000. Notice the effect on net profit of this change in cost of sales.

Figure 8-7
Projected Income Statement with Change in Cost of Sales

Fiesta Bicycle Shop
Projected Income Statement
For Year Ended December 31, 19--

	Change in Cost of Sales	Original Estimate
Sales (1,000 units @ $100)	$100,000	$100,000
Cost of Sales (1,000 units @ $57)	57,000	60,000
Gross Profit	43,000	40,000
Operating Expenses	35,000	35,000
Net Profit	$ 8,000	$ 5,000

As a result of a 5 percent decrease in the cost of each unit sold, Fiesta Bicycle Shop's owners would see their net profit change from $5,000 to $8,000, an increase of 60 percent.

A CHANGE IN OPERATING EXPENSES

A fourth way to increase net profit is to reduce operating expenses. Assume that the owners of Fiesta Bicycle Shop have studied every operating expense, such as wages, salaries, and rent, and they have decided that they could reduce some of those expenses to save $5,000 during the year. Most of the savings would come from reducing the number of hours worked by their part-time employees and working more hours themselves. As shown in Figure 8-8, on page 196, the $5,000 reduction in operating expenses results in a $5,000 increase in net profit.

When other factors remain the same, net profit increases with:

1. An increase in price.
2. An increase in volume.
3. A decrease in cost of sales.
4. A decrease in operating expenses.

With the exception of sales volume, which is accompanied by a change in cost of sales, the other variables operate independently of one another. That is, a change in one variable does not affect another variable.

Figure 8-8
Projected Income Statement with Change in Operating Expenses

Fiesta Bicycle Shop
Projected Income Statement
For Year Ended December 31, 19--

	Change in Operating Expenses	Original Estimate
Sales (1,000 units @ $100)	$100,000	$100,000
Cost of Sales (1,000 units @ $60)	60,000	60,000
Gross Profit	40,000	40,000
Operating Expenses	30,000	35,000
Net Profit	$ 10,000	$ 5,000

ACTION STEPS FOR ASPIRING ENTREPRENEURS

Use these action steps to help you prepare for the possibility of being an entrepreneur at some point in your career:

1. Choose a tentative date for starting your enterprise. It may be next week, next year, or a few years away. The important thing is that you give yourself a target date.
2. Plan what you will be doing between now and the day you begin your new enterprise. In your plan, include the work experience and further schooling that will help you prepare for a career in entrepreneurship.
3. Start saving your money and preparing yourself financially to create your own enterprise.
4. Use your business plan as a guide in reaching your goal of becoming an entrepreneur.

BUILDING YOUR ENTERPRISE VOCABULARY

Match the following terms with the statements that best define those terms. Write the letter of your choice in the space provided.

a. cash balance
b. cash receipts
c. projected income statement
d. net profit
e. gross profit
f. balance sheet
g. accounts receivable
h. intangible assets
i. net worth
j. volume

_______ 1. A picture of the assets and the claims against those assets.
_______ 2. Cash on hand.
_______ 3. Customers owe the business.
_______ 4. Includes cash sales, collection of credit sales, and loans.
_______ 5. Number of units sold.
_______ 6. What remains after all expenses, including taxes, are paid.
_______ 7. Based on estimates of sales, cost of sales, and expenses.
_______ 8. Do not exist in a physical sense.
_______ 9. Includes money invested by owners.
_______ 10. Sales minus cost of sales.

UNDERSTANDING KEY CONCEPTS

Write a short answer to each of the questions below.

1. What financial statements should be included in the business plan?

____

____

____

2. Write out the cash budget formula.

3. Show how the parts of an income statement are related.

4. Explain why one type of financial statement is called a balance sheet.

___

___

5. Describe each of the four basic profit variables.

___

___

___

___

___

APPLYING YOUR ENTERPRISE KNOWLEDGE

These activities will give you a chance to apply what you have learned in Chapter 8.

1. Based on your own experience, and also by asking relatives and friends, identify three business firms in your community that have lowered their prices in an attempt to sell a larger volume of products or services. In the space provided, write the name of each business and answer the questions.

   a. Name of business: ___

   What is the main line of products or services offered by the business?

   ___

   Are the prices charged by the business lower than those of its competitors? ___

   If yes, how much lower are the prices? ___

   Why do people buy from this business? ___

   ___

   ___

b. Name of business: ______________________

What is the main line of products or services offered by the business?

____

Are the prices charged by the business lower than those of its competitors? ______________________

If yes, how much lower are the prices? ______________________

Why do people buy from this business? ______________________

____

____

c. Name of business: ______________________

What is the main line of products or services offered by the business?

____

Are the prices charged by the business lower than those of its competitors? ______________________

If yes, how much lower are the prices? ______________________

Why do people buy from this business? ______________________

____

____

2. Identify some methods that businesses in your community have used to reduce their expenses. You may have to ask relatives for their help with this activity.

____

____

____

____

SOLVING BUSINESS PROBLEMS: UNFINISHED FURNITURE MANUFACTURING COMPANY

The Ryans have just finished their first year in business. They manufacture and sell unfinished wood furniture. A sizable market segment exists consisting of people who prefer to finish the furniture themselves. Judging by their first year's income statement, the Ryans feel they are doing a good job of serving that market. A shortened form of the income statement is as shown on page 200:

Ryans' Unfinished Furniture Manufacturing Company Income Statement For Year Ended December 31, 19–	
Sales	$487,100
Cost of Sales	306,873
Gross Profit	180,227
Operating Expenses	165,614
Net Profit	$ 14,613

The Ryans are pleased that their company made enough money the first year to pay their salaries and also earn a profit. Looking ahead to their second year in business, the Ryans want to increase sales and the percentage of net profit earned on sales.

Assume that the Ryans have asked you to assist them in determining how the basic profit variables affect net profit.

1. How would a 5 percent increase in prices affect net profit? Assume all other factors remain the same. Show your answer in both dollar and percentage terms.

2. What is the effect on net profit of a 5 percent reduction in cost of sales? Assume all other factors remain the same. Show your answer in both dollar and percentage terms. (Round to the nearest dollar and nearest percent.)

3. Show the effect on net profit of a 5 percent reduction in operating expenses. Assume all other factors remain the same. Show your answer in both dollar and percentage terms. (Round to the nearest dollar and nearest percent.)

4. How would the following changes affect net profit if they are made at the same time: prices are increased by 2 percent, cost of sales is reduced by 2 percent, and operating expenses are reduced by 2 percent? Show your answer in both dollar and percentage terms. (Round to the nearest dollar and nearest percent.)

BUSINESS PLAN PROJECT

Use the space provided on pages 203–205 for the business plan activities below. Write the name of your enterprise on the blank line at the top of each form.

1. Prepare a cash budget for your first twelve months in business.

2. Prepare a projected income statement for the first year of your new enterprise.

3. Prepare a balance sheet showing assets, liabilities, and capital just prior to opening.

The "Business Plan Project" sections from all eight chapters comprise a complete business plan for your new enterprise.

CASH BUDGET
January–December, 19--

	Month 1	Month 2	Month 3	Month 4	Month 5	Month 6	Month 7	Month 8	Month 9	Month 10	Month 11	Month 12
Beginning Cash Balance												
Cash Receipts: Cash Sales												
Credit Sales Payments . . .												
Loans												
Total Cash Available												
Total Cash Disbursements for the Month . .												
Cash Balance at End of Month . .												

PROJECTED INCOME STATEMENT
For Year Ended December 31, 19–

Sales		$ ________
Cost of Sales		________
Gross Profit		$ ________
Expenses		
Wages and Salaries	$ ________	
Rent	________	
Advertising and Sales Promotion	________	
Delivery Expenses	________	
Supplies and Materials	________	
Utilities	________	
Insurance	________	
Taxes (but not federal income tax)	________	
Interest on Debt	________	
Repairs and Maintenance	________	
Fees for Accountants and Lawyers	________	
Employee Training Costs	________	
Other Expenses	________	
Total Expenses		$ ________
Net Profit (before income tax)		$ ________

____

BALANCE SHEET
December 31, 19–

Assets		
Current Assets:		
Cash	$ ________	
Inventory	________	
Accounts Receivable	________	
Total Current Assets		$ ________
Fixed Assets:		
Land	$ ________	
Building	________	
Equipment	________	
Total Fixed Assets		________
Intangible Assets:		
Goodwill	$ ________	
Other Intangible Assets	________	
Total Intangible Assets		________
Total Assets		$ ________
Liabilities		
Current Liabilities:		
Accounts Payable	$ ________	
Notes Payable	________	
Accrued Expenses	________	
Total Current Liabilities		$ ________
Fixed Liabilities:		
Long-Term Loan	$ ________	
Mortgage	________	
Total Fixed Liabilities		________
Total Liabilities		$ ________
Net Worth		
Owner's Capital		________
Total Liabilities and Net Worth		$ ________

GLOSSARY

A

Accessory equipment. Equipment such as hand tools and electric floor sweepers used in operating a business.

Accounts payable. Amounts that an enterprise owes to suppliers for goods and services provided.

Accounts receivable. Sums of money owed to the business by customers.

Accounts receivable loans. Loans involving the pledging of accounts receivable as collateral for a short-term bank loan.

Accrued expenses. Expenses incurred but not yet paid.

Acquirers. People who become entrepreneurs by buying an existing business.

Advertising. Any nonpersonal presentation of information about products or services that is paid for by an identified sponsor.

Advertising copy. The written or spoken words of an advertising message.

Agents. In the distribution channel, those who assist in the sale of products without owning the products.

Articles of partnership. A written agreement among the members of a partnership.

Assets. Items or possessions used in a business that have monetary value.

Average market share. Market potential divided by the number of competing businesses.

B

Balance sheet. A financial statement showing what an enterprise owns, what it owes, and what the owner has invested.

Brainstorming. A problem-solving technique that involves generating as many ideas as possible.

Business closure. Going out of business for any reason.

Business expenses. Ordinary and necessary costs of operating a business.

Business failure. Closing a business while money is owed to at least one creditor.

Business income. Total dollars received for all goods and services sold during the year.

Business knowledge. Knowing how to operate the enterprise.

Business opportunity advertisements. Advertisements offering businesses for sale.

Business plan. A written description of every part of a new enterprise.

Business services. *See* Industrial services.

Business services advertisements. Advertisements placed by persons with specialized business or technical skills to sell.

Business users. Companies or institutions that buy products and services to use in running their businesses, to resell, to produce other products, or to provide services.

Buy-sell artists. Entrepreneurs who buy a business and then sell it at a higher price.

C

Capital aggregators. Entrepreneurs who take the lead in pulling together the large amounts of capital needed to start enterprises.

Cash balance. Cash on hand and in the bank as of a particular date.

Cash budget. A measure of changes in the cash an enterprise will have available from month to month.

Cash disbursements. An estimate of cash that will have to be paid out during a specified period for purchases and for operating or continuing expenses.

Cash receipts. An estimate of all funds that will be received from cash sales, collection of credit sales, and loans during a specified period.

Channel of distribution. The path a product follows from the producer to consumers or business users.

Charter. A written document outlining the conditions under which a corporation will operate.

Classified advertising. Advertising messages grouped together in one part of the newspaper; often called want ads.

Collateral. Something of value pledged to a bank by a borrower as security for a loan.

Commercial finance companies. Companies that specialize in accounts receivable and inventory loans.

Commercial loan. A short-term bank loan to a business, usually made for 90 to 180 days.

Compensating balance. A sum of money deposited in a bank for the duration of a loan to serve as collateral.

Compensation. Wages and salaries paid to employees.

Competition. The effort of two or more businesses to win the same group of people as customers.

Competitors. Individual firms trying to win the same group of people as customers.

Conservative expense estimate. An expense estimate that is more likely to be too high than too low.

Conservative sales estimate. A sales estimate that is more likely to be too low than too high.

Consumer products. Products that individuals and families buy for their personal use.

Consumer services. Tasks individuals and families pay others to do or provide for them.

Consumer's viewpoint. A view of products and services in terms of the benefits derived from their use.

Consumers. Persons or households that buy products and services for personal or family use.

Continuing costs. Costs that will be incurred throughout the life of an enterprise, such as rent and telephone service.

Convenience goods. Inexpensive items that consumers buy often and with little shopping effort.

Corporation. An enterprise having the legal rights, duties, and powers of a person.

Cost of goods manufactured. Term used in manufacturing for cost of sales.

Cost of goods sold. Term used by retailers and wholesalers for cost of sales.

Cost of sales. The cost of the products or services sold in a given time period.

Cost of services sold. In a service business, may be a calculation based on wages paid to persons providing the service.

Craft and hobby shows. Places where people show others what they make or study in their spare time.

Creativity. The ability to visualize and implement new ideas.

Credit. The privilege of paying for goods and services after they have been delivered or provided.

Current assets. Cash and any other assets that can be easily and quickly turned into cash; current assets are those an enterprise would not expect to hold longer than one year.

Current liabilities. Debts that are due to be paid in one year or less.

Customer services. The extra benefits that a business provides for its customers.

Debt funds. Borrowed dollars or capital.

Delivered cost of goods. The cost of the merchandise itself plus shipping costs.

Direct retailing. Retailing in which the salesperson goes to the home of the consumer with products or samples.

Double taxation. Taxing business profits twice; under the corporate form of organization, the corporation must pay taxes on its profits and stockholders must pay personal income taxes on their share of the same profits.

Economy-of-large-scale exploiters. Entrepreneurs who can sell a large volume of goods at reduced prices.

Employee benefits. Benefits such as health insurance, paid vacations, and pensions provided to employees in addition to regular compensation to attract and keep a good work force.

Enterprise. An establishment that supplies us with products and services in exchange for payment; also referred to as a business or a business enterprise.

Entrepreneur. A person who attempts to earn a profit by taking the risk of operating a business.

Entrepreneurship. The act or process of getting into and managing your own business enterprise.

Equipment leasing. An arrangement whereby individuals may obtain and use equipment without owning it.

Equipment loans. Loans that enable an enterprise to buy new equipment or to obtain funds when the firm does not qualify for unsecured credit.

Equity. Ownership.

Equity funds. Money or capital contributed to a business by its owners.

Established clientele. A group of regular customers who are in the habit of buying goods and services from the enterprise.

Ethics. A set of rules that defines right and wrong conduct.

Existing business. A business that is already set up.

Expenses. All the costs of running an enterprise other than those included in the cost of sales.

Exporting. The sale and shipping of products manufactured in one country to customers in another country.

Extractive enterprises. Enterprises that grow products or take raw materials from where they are found in nature.

F

Factoring. Selling accounts receivable to obtain short-term funds.

Factors. Financial firms that buy accounts receivable.

Financial planning. A means by which a business plan can be described in terms of dollars.

First mortgage. Security for a real estate loan.

Fixed assets. Items a business expects to own for more than one year—for example, land and buildings.

Fixed liabilities. Debts that are due to be paid in more than a year; also called long-term liabilities.

Formal survey. A survey that involves either interviewing many people or asking them to complete a questionnaire.

Franchise. A legal agreement or contract between a company and an entrepreneur who will sell the company's goods or services in a given area.

Franchisee. An entrepreneur who contracts to sell a franchisor's goods or services in a certain area.

Franchisor. A manufacturer, wholesaler, or service company that sells its product or service through entrepreneurs.

General partnership. The common type of partnership, in which all partners have unlimited liability for the enterprise's debts.

Goal. An objective; something you plan to achieve.

Goodwill. The extra money that would have to be paid to buy an enterprise because it has a good reputation.

Gross margin. Gross profit stated as a percentage.

Gross profit. What remains after cost of sales is subtracted from sales.

Hiring. The process of deciding whether a prospective employee is suitable for the job.

Hobbies. Activities pursued for pleasure and relaxation.

Home-based business. A full-time or part-time enterprise that produces goods or services operating in or from the home.

Human resource management. Activities directed toward building a motivated and effective work force.

Ill will. A feeling of hostility.

Image. How customers feel about doing business with an enterprise.

Importing. Buying products in another country and bringing them into one's own country.

Income statement. A statement showing how a business has performed over a certain period of time; also called a profit-and-loss statement.

Independence. Freedom from the control of others.

Independent innovators. Individuals who create companies to manufacture and sell products they have invented.

Industrial distributors. Wholesalers who buy products from manufacturers and sell them to industrial users.

Industrial products. Products that one business buys from another business.

Industrial services. Tasks one business pays another business to perform for it; also called business services.

Industry. All the firms that offer a particular product or service.

Informal survey. A survey conducted by talking to one's family and friends.

Initial fee. The down payment made by the franchisee when the franchise is purchased.

Innovative. Having the imagination to think of new products or new ways of doing things.

Installations. Major items used to produce a product (e.g., printing presses) or to provide a service (e.g., jet airplanes).

Institutional advertising. Advertising that focuses on the enterprise itself and is designed to create a favorable image and build goodwill.

Intangible assets. Assets that have value and are useful to an enterprise but do not exist in a physical sense.

Interest. A charge involved in borrowing money or using credit.

Intermediaries. Businesses that aid in transferring goods from the producer to the user.

International business. The transacting of business and commercial activity across national boundaries.

Inventory. Raw materials, finished goods, or supplies on hand.

Inventory financing. An arrangement whereby an entrepreneur pledges inventory to a commercial bank as collateral for short-term funds to receive a revolving line of credit.

Invested capital. The entrepreneur's capital used in starting the enterprise.

J

Job security. The assurance of continuing employment and income.

Laws. Values or standards of society that are enforceable through the courts.

Liabilities. The debts of an enterprise.

Licensing. In international business, an arrangement whereby a foreign firm obtains the rights to make and sell a product in its country and to pay a percentage of each sale to the original company.

Limited control. Lack of freedom to make all the decisions for the business that an independent entrepreneur normally makes; a disadvantage of being a franchisee.

Limited life. A term referring to the fact that a sole proprietorship is tied to the life of the owner and will be dissolved upon the death, imprisonment, or bankruptcy of the proprietor.

Long-term liabilities. *See* Fixed liabilities.

M

Mail-order retailing. Retailing in which customers order the goods they want from catalogs or advertisements.

Management difficulty. Problems resulting in a sole proprietorship because one person carries the burden of managing the business alone.

Managing. Seeing to it that the day-to-day tasks in operating a business are performed appropriately.

Manufacturing businesses. Businesses that take raw materials and change them into a form that consumers can use.

Market. Groups of people, businesses, or organizations seeking certain types of products or services.

Market potential. The total sales of all similar businesses in a particular area.

Market segmentation. Dividing the market for a product or service into segments.

Market segments. Groups of people with similar needs and characteristics.

Marketing. A set of business activities that provides products and services to satisfy consumer needs and wants.

Marketing concept. A way of thinking about a business in terms of consumer needs and wants.

Marketing strategy. Methods used by an enterprise to reach its target market.

Markup. The amount that is added to the cost of an item in arriving at the selling price.

Media. The carriers of an advertising message, such as newspapers, radio, magazines, and television.

Moderate risk. A chance of winning that is neither too small nor too great.

Multinational corporation. A business enterprise that has significant operations in several countries.

N

Net profit. Income remaining after paying all expenses, including taxes.

Net worth. The excess of the value of the assets over the value of the liabilities.

Notes payable. Short-term loans that have to be repaid within a year.

One-time costs. Expenses that will not have to be repeated once the business is under way.

Organization chart. A diagram showing how one job in an enterprise fits in with others.

Organizing. The process of gathering the money, people, and machinery needed to get a business started.

Over-the-counter retailing. The most common form of retailing, it involves having a store where customers come to shop and buy what they want from the retailer's stock.

Owner's capital. All money invested in a business by its owners.

Partnership. A business enterprise owned by two or more persons.

Parts. Items incorporated into a finished product with little or no change.

Pattern multipliers. Entrepreneurs who build several units of an effective business.

Penetration pricing policy. The policy of setting a low initial price for a new product or service to attract customers quickly.

Personal guarantees. Agreements by borrowers to pay the unpaid balance of a loan if the business is unable to repay it.

Personal satisfaction. Doing what you want with your life.

Personal selling. Direct contact between a salesperson and a customer.

Physical facilities. Buildings and parking lots or driveways.

Price. The exchange value of products and services stated in terms of money.

Probable-case scenario. An outline of a chain of events that describes what is likely to occur in a particular situation.

Processed materials. Products that are produced by one business, but will be changed into another form by other businesses.

Product advertising. Advertising that features specific products and services for the purpose of creating immediate sales.

Products. Tangible items—things you can touch, such as clothing, furniture, and cosmetics; also called goods.

Profit. The amount of sales income left after all expenses have been paid.

Profit-and-loss statement. *See* Income statement.

Projected income statement. A statement based on estimates of sales, cost of sales, and expenses for the first year of a new enterprise's operation.

Promotion. Activities directed at informing customers about products and services being offered for sale and persuading them to buy.

Proven record. A record of having earned a profit for the current owner of the business.

Public shows. Places where manufacturers and distributors display and demonstrate their products to the public.

Quantity discount. A reduction in price as a result of the amount purchased.

R

Raw materials. Products that are in their natural state when businesses buy them.

Real estate loans. Loans usually made for up to 75 percent of the value of the particular land and/or buildings and repaid over 10 to 20 years.

Retailers. Those who buy products from wholesalers, manufacturers, or extractive enterprises and sell them to customers.

Revolving line of credit. An arrangement whereby funds are continually advanced by a commercial bank to a business borrower, repaid, and advanced once again.

Royalty. The fee paid by the franchisee for the life of the franchise.

Salaries. Fixed dollar amounts paid regularly, such as weekly or monthly, to employees.

Sales. All income that flows into the business from sales activity.

Sales forecast. An estimate of sales, in dollars or units, for a specified period of time.

Sales promotion. All activities designed to build sales by supplementing advertising and personal selling.

Scenario. An outline of a chain of events that an individual believes could possibly occur in the future.

Self-confidence. The belief that you can achieve what you set out to do.

Seller's viewpoint. A narrow definition that sees products only as physical objects and services only as tasks performed.

Services. Tasks we pay others to do or provide for us.

Shopping goods. Items that people buy after comparing the price, quality, and other features of similar items.

Sideline business. A business started after regular work hours or on weekends during other employment.

Skimming pricing policy. The policy of charging a relatively high price for a new product or service to try to recover as soon as possible the cost of developing the product.

Small business. A business enterprise that is independently owned and operated and is not one of the major companies in its field of business activity.

Small business management. The process of operating a small business.

Sole proprietorship. An enterprise owned by only one person.

Solo self-employed individuals. Entrepreneurs who work alone or with only a few employees.

Special-interest magazines. Magazines devoted to a specific area of interest, such as camping or biking.

Specialized management. Assigning different management functions to different people; an advantage of the corporate form of organization.

Specialty goods. Products that consumers will make a special effort to buy.

Starting from scratch. Doing all the work of establishing an enterprise.

Status. A person's social rank or position.

Stock. Shares of ownership in a corporation.

Stockholders. The owners of a corporation.

Supplies. Items that aid in a firm's operations but do not become a part of the finished product.

Survey. A way of gathering information that involves asking a number of people questions and then summarizing their answers.

T

Target market. The particular group at which a product or service is directed.

Team builders. Entrepreneurs who expand small, usually one-person businesses into larger companies.

Technical knowledge. Necessary knowledge about a product or service.

Term loans. Loans extended for more than one year and used to obtain land, buildings, equipment, and other fixed assets.

Trade association. A group of businesses that have joined together to benefit a particular line of business.

Trade credit. An arrangement offered by vendors whereby entrepreneurs may have 30 or more days to pay their bills for merchandise.

Trade publications. Magazines and newspapers designed for people working within a particular business or field.

Trade shows. Exhibits of products from many suppliers organized by groups of manufacturers and wholesalers; open only to people engaged in a particular line of business or trade.

Training. Activities directed toward equipping employees with the skills they need to do the job effectively.

U

Unlimited liability. Personal liability for all business debts; a disadvantage of the sole proprietorship and partnership forms of business organization.

V

Vending machine retailing. Retailing in which the customer deposits money in a machine and receives the goods immediately.

Vendors. Businesses from which entrepreneurs buy products.

Volume. With respect to sales, the number of units of a product sold.

Voluntary closure. Closing a business because one wishes to do something else.

Wages. Payments to workers on an hourly basis.

Wholesalers. Those who buy goods from extractive or manufacturing enterprises and sell them to other businesses.

Worst-case scenario. An outline of a chain of events in which one imagines a situation as bad as it could get.

INDEX

D

E

F

G

M

N

O

P

Q

R

S

T